THE
TOMMY COOPER
JOKE BOOK

Compiled by JOHN FISHER

6 8 10 9 7

Arrow Books
20 Vauxhall Bridge Road
London SW1V 2SA

Arrow Books is part of the Penguin Random House group of companies whose
addresses can be found at global.penguinrandomhouse.com

Penguin
Random House
UK

First published as *The Tommy Cooper Joke Book* in 2009 and *Tommy Cooper's
Secret Joke Files* in 2011 in Great Britain by Preface Publishing
Published in paperback by Arrow Books in 2014

www.penguin.co.uk

A CIP catalogue record for this book is available from the British Library.

ISBN 780099557661

Designed and artworked by Andy Spence Design
www.andyspence.co.uk

Penguin Random House is committed to a sustainable future for our business,
our readers and our planet. This book is made from Forest Stewardship
Council® certified paper.

MIX
Paper from
responsible sources
FSC® C018179

Printed and bound in Italy by L.E.G.O. S.p.A. Lavis (TN)

'JOKES ARE LIKE TRICKS...'

An introduction by John Fisher

It is twenty-five years since Tommy Cooper died the most visible of deaths live on television on the stage of Her Majesty's Theatre in London's West End. Unwittingly a showman till the end, he kept the audience in suspense as his gangling bulk crumpled beneath a voluminous scarlet and gold lamé cloak in the manner of the master stage illusionists of his youth. Visually it seemed the prelude to the most spectacular of vanishing tricks and he would have relished the expectation that fell upon the audience before the grim reality dawned. In the same way he would have loved the hint of contradiction in that first sentence. One can hear him now proclaiming, 'Dead, live. Live, dead.' He had a way with words – teasing their meaning, relishing their ambiguity, falling foul of their pitfalls – in a manner that was as joyous as his way with the pedestrian props of the magician's trade. 'Egg, bag. Bag, egg.' 'Bottle, glass. Glass, bottle.'

No one who saw or heard Cooper ever forgot him and since his death the status of folk hero he acquired in his lifetime has become raised to an even higher level as new generations have caught up with his comedy through technology that once would have appeared to be real magic. It is well documented how Tommy took his first step on the road to acclaim as the world's most successful worst wizard, when the milk in the bottle refused to defy the law of gravity at a concert he gave in a works canteen when a shipyard apprentice just outside Southampton in his late teens. After the initial sting of disappointment, the not-displeasing sound of laughter that then greeted his misfortune had a life-transforming effect on him. Magic tricks began to be chosen with their built-in laughter potential in mind. More importantly jokes and gags that did not need props soon became grist to the comedic mill, not least when war called and the scope for entertaining his army chums was restricted by his inability to carry anything but the lightest of magical apparatus in his kitbag. His stage shows would follow the pattern of tricks and gags – 'Gag, trick. Trick, gag' – until the end of his days.

Ironically, although everyone has a favourite memory of Cooper attemptingto purvey his hocus-pocus craft, what people remember most affectionately about him are the funny lines that, whatever their origin, needed only him to say them to be stamped with his copyright for evermore. It seemed, therefore, an appropriate way to mark the silver anniversary of his death to compile this volume. While not pretending to be encyclopaedic, it represents a comprehensive anthology of most of his familiar stand-up material and much else besides. I almost wrote 'familial' there and one is reminded that the original meaning of the earlier word was one of just such family intimacy. The jokes themselves have become old friends and achieve their greatest effect when told – preferably with a Cooper voice and Cooper gestures – amongst near ones and dear ones, the safest short-cut to hilarity at a family dinner table at celebratory times of the year. Cooper's radiant warmth and instant rapport as a performer informed his telling of them and I am sure that in any poll of recent entertainers whom the public at large might wish to invite to such a gathering, he would come in miles ahead of the rest of the pack. Not that Cooper could have been any card but the Joker, the rightful court jester in a monarchy where, as these pages will show, he entranced both the ruler and her subjects.

By contrast, away from the spotlight and the public gaze, Cooper was a serious man. To watch him fret over the fine detail of an exploding piece of magic apparatus or worry over the disposition of the crazy props on his table just before he sauntered on stage was to discern a perfectionist that might have put Fred Astaire to shame. His attitude to comedy was no less punctilious, although it surprises many people to discover that he did not write his own material – at least not the ninety-nine per cent that failed to qualify as instant ad-lib forged in the heat of performance and seldom paraded again until the same circumstances prevailed. Today performers on the comedy circuit are to a large extent regarded as *persona non grata* if they are not recognised as the originators of their material. In Tommy's time everyone took for granted that Bob Hope had a battalion of joke writers and that Tony Hancock was a lesser animal when deprived of a Galton and Simpson script. And yet so intense and persuasive was the persona of the genial fez-capped zany that people assumed automatically that he was a creative genius – which he was, of course, but in other ways entirely.

Within his own resources the young Cooper went to extreme lengths to ensure that nothing missed his attention. He was introduced to joke-book culture as a performer through the slender pamphlets written by Robert Orben, a slick American comedywriter who happened also to be a professional magician. These slender tomes could be picked up readily over the counters of the best magic shops in London. Many of the lines were linked to established magic tricks, many were stand-alone one-liners. The booklets in their gaudy soft paper covers flaunted themselves under titles like 'Patter Parade', 'Laugh Package', 'Bits, Boffs and Banter' and 'Screamline Comedy.'

To a top professional funny man the outlay of fourteen shillings was considered a sound investment if only one workable gag was forthcoming from the pages purchased. However, the popularity of the books within the comedy profession led to the over-familiarity of much of their contents. Lenny Bruce once advertised a performance with the tag line, 'No Joe Miller (a reference to the morose eighteenth century actor whose name became synonymous with stale humour), no corn, no Orben.' Orben threatened to sue, though never did. In his later years he would become speech writer to President Gerald Ford, providing a quirky footnote to American political history in a way that none of his comedy customers of the forties and fifties could have envisaged.

Tommy soon realised he needed something a little more exclusive and in the early fifties found the solution on a visit to New York where he became acquainted with Billy Glason, an ex-vaudevillian who had travelled America with an act billed as 'Just Songs and Sayings.' To keep boredom at bay on the relentless circuit away from home, old pros notoriously turned to booze, broads, or golf. Glason was the exception and appears to have kept himself out of mischief by compiling on index cards files of every joke he ever heard. When he retired from the stage, he set to and began to reorder this material, often twisting and adapting it to keep pace with the times. Ed Sullivan, Johnny Carson, Steve Allen, even Bob Hope began to avail themselves of his services. Tommy found himself to be the lucky Briton in the right place at the right time, one of the privileged few granted purchase of Glason's gargantuan twenty-six part 'Fun-Master Giant Encyclopaedia of Classified Gags.' In the days before photo-copying became commonplace, the material was published on the thinnest paper possible, 'to make it possible to make as many carbon copies as we can!' What Glason lost on the number of copies, however, his purchasers made up for in exclusivity. The work is reputed to have been advertised originally for three thousand dollars, although the paperwork in Cooper's files shows that he paid a knockdown price of nine hundred. It was still a lot of money over fifty years ago.

Over the next few years Tommy acquired much more from Glason, including the five volumes of his 'Book of Blackouts', the three of his 'Book of Parodies', the nine lessons of his 'Comedy and Emcee Lecture Book', not to mention his 'Humor-Dor for Emcees and Comedians.' In bulk this material, all published under Glason's 'Fun-Master' imprint, must approximate to the combined capacity of the accumulated telephone directories amassed by the average individual in a couple of lifetimes. Cooper also subscribed to a monthly sheet issued by Billy entitled simply 'The Comedian.' Similar bulletins of gag material were issued by two more New Yorkers, Art Paul's 'Punch Lines' and Eddie Gay's 'Gay's Gags.' The British scriptwriter Peter Cagney followed suit with his own newsletter. They all fell through the Cooper letter box. To peruse his copies today is tantamount to being perched on his shoulder as he scrupulously read each gag and marked those that appealed accordingly. Not that the marks predominate. There was just so much to choose from.

Tommy's favourite bedtime reading.

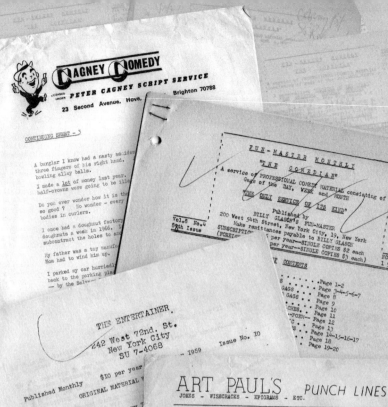

CAGNEY COMEDY
PETER CAGNEY SCRIPT SERVICE
23 Second Avenue, Hove. Brighton 70788

CONTINUING SHEET - 3

A burglar I know had a nasty accident.... three fingers of his right hand.... bowling alley balls.

I made a lot of money last year.... half-crowns were going to be ille....

Do you ever wonder how it is th.... so good ? No wonder - every.... bodies in curlers.

I once had a doughnut factory.... doughnuts a week in 1966. I.... subcontract the holes to and....

My father was a toy manufa.... Mom had to wind him up.

I parked my car hurriedly.... back to the parking pla.... — by the Salv——

FUN-MASTER MONTHLY
"THE COMEDIAN"
A service of PROFESSIONAL COMEDY MATERIAL consisting of
Gags of the DAY, WEEK and MONTH
"THE ONLY SERVICE OF ITS KIND"

Published by
BILLY GLASON'S FUN-MASTER
200 West 54th Street, New York City, 19, New York
Make remittances payable to BILLY GLASON
SUBSCRIPTION....per year——SINGLE COPIES $2 each
(FOREIGN....per year——SINGLE COPIES $3 each)

Vol.8 No.4
59th Issue

NOVEMBER
1957

CONTENTS
....Page 1-2
GAGS ....Page 3-4-5-6-7
GAGS ....Page 8
....Page 9
....Page 10
....Page 11
(POEM)....Page 12
....Page 13
....Page 14-15-16-17
....Page 18
....Page 19-20

THE ENTERTAINER
242 West 72nd. St.
New York City
SU 7-4068

Issue No. 10
1959

Published Monthly $10 per year

ORIGINAL MATERIAL W....

THANKSGIVING

1 I really got a bargain on my T....
   drumsticks were bigger than t....

2 Nelson Rockefeller has a lot....
   his grandfather gave away a....
   Nelson.

3 King Farouk had a lovely T....
   with his drumstick.
   ....wing has....

ART PAUL'S PUNCH LINES
JOKES - WISECRACKS - EPIGRAMS - ETC.
No. 4

* What about the deformed cows....have bags under their eyes.
* My doctor said I had a good color....he was looking at the greenbacks in my wallet.
* I bought a watch F-O-B instead of a chain..and some fish from Massachusetts, C-O-D.
* Double wedding in Kentucky....two shotguns.
* I know a baseball Umps who's running a lunch room....the other morning I ordered wheat cakes....he shouted to his cook, "Batter up"
* Was out to my uncle's chicken ranch for Sunday dinner....you'd think I came over in the Mayflower the way I landed on that Plymouth Rock.
* He's a graduate of the Sch.... of Hard Knocks...only they all hit him in the head.
* I heard.... ....er shortage that the counterfeiters have a hard
....partment store ever had...He's so crosseyed nobody
....ur sizes....small, medium large and do you see
....old one painted over
....nds call him Bacon....somebody is always bringing
....night. We were sitting on the sofa when she
....t. I went home...I can take a hint.
....If you hear a suspicious noise at night, just
....umerals.
....stealing kisses right under the girls' noses.
....k at her, time stands still. She's got a face
....n trying to straighten out the Pretzel business
....e okay when his new teeth come in.
....to pay his rent. Pay his rent! I can't even

GAY'S GAGS
242 West 72nd St.
New York 23, N.Y.

PUBLISHED MONTHLY $12 PER YEAR   OCTOBER 1963   ISSUE NO. 58
(Two year subscription $20) BARGAIN RATES ON BACK ISSUES: 6 back issues
(latest) $5; 12 back issues (latest) $9; 40 back issues (first) $20

ORIGINAL MATERIAL WRITTEN BY EDDIE GAY

THANKSGIVING.....SURPLUS WHEAT:.....MADAME NHU:.....BOBBY BAKER:

I have one thing to be thankful for this Thanksgiving----I
didn't have to pay for the turkey....After looking at my mother-in-law's
face over Thanksgiving weekend I know the frost is on the pumpkin....he
JFK has a lot to be thankful for this Thanksgiving----he didn't find any
surplus wheat in his turkey stuffing.....Even though Thanksgiving has
been over for two weeks Goldwater, JFK and Rocky are still hanging on
to their wishbone.....I can tell Thanksgiving is coming----my relatives
have been camped outside the house since Labor Day....It was a great
day for the family----we had so many relatives at our table the Fire
Department insisted on stationing a fireman in the parlor....I paid $20
for a turkey----I think I got taken----it tasted like it was older than
Thanksgiving....The frost is on the pumpkin--in Republican language
that means JFK's Civil Rights legislation is being watered down....The
Kennedys played touch football after their Thanksgiving dinner....JFK
dropped a touchdown pass in the end zone from Bobby when he couldn't let
go of his wishbone....At first JFK couldn't make up his mind about who
to sell our surplus wheat too----Russia or Jack Armstrong.....Will Russ-
ia pay us for World War II....we had two old turkeys this year----
they owe us from World War II....we had two old turkeys this year----
one on top of the table and one sitting at it----my mother-in-law.
It's a good idea to sell our surplus wheat----in this country we
can use the money----to raise more surplus wheat....At first JFK band de-
....everything but the Treasury....ellars. Sell all our gold and use the
....advised him

"THE COMEDIAN" for JANUARY, 1959
Vol.9 No.6 (102nd issue) Page -4-

MORE ONE-LINERS (continued -2-)

He wasn't bald, his head just grew up through his hair!

My act got a wonderful review--in "POPULAR MECHANICS".

My golf is sure improving. I'm missing the ball much closer than I used to.

It isn't the line you GIVE a gal that BOTHERS her, it's the PAWS in between!

I don't know where my next dollar's coming from but my wife already knows where it's going!

She's always making mountains out of moth-balls!

When I was born I was so fat my Mother had to jack me up to change my diapers! (or: when HE was born, etc.)

I gave my girl a cultured pearl set--a dozen oysters and a knife!

Boy, was that restaurant expensive! I said to the Waiter: "Haven't you got any slightly used steaks?"

Before I leave I have some advice for you people who have trouble falling asleep. Drink a pint of rye before you go to bed. S L E E P   T I G H T!

I got a one-man dog...he only bites ME!

Everytime he gets a raise his wife gets a new hat. His success seems to go to HER head!

You can always cure your husband's snoring by kindness, good advice, friendly cooperation--and by STUFFING AN OLD SOCK IN HIS MOUTH!

You can always tell who the Boss is. He's the one who watches the clock during the coffee break!

Marriage is a union that allows a husband to work for a Boss without PAY!

Early to bed and early to rise, till you make enough money to do otherwise!

Tommy strikes lucky!

(NEXT PAGE)

GAY'S GAGS
242 West 72nd St.
New York 23, N.Y.
OCTOBER 1963   ISSUE NO. 58
BACK ISSUES: 6 back issues
(first) $20.

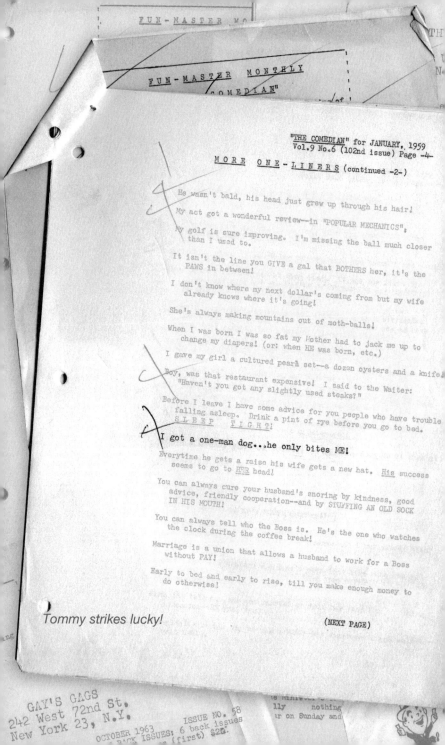

They always tell you to be ready when Opportunity knocks!. Well, one night I was ready,when somebody knocked and spoiled a beautiful opportunity!

Why do they rave so much about Marilyn Monroe? Take away her sexy look and her terrific figure and what have ya got? MY WIFE!

Even though he's wealthy now he's never forgotten his poor childhood on the lower East Side. Once a month he goes back there to visit his wife and kids!

When I asked her to have something to eat, she said "I file for a great big steak, what do YOU file for?" I said "I file for bankruptcy!"

I told the waiter the cup was dirty and he said "You're crazy, that's not dirt, that's only lipstick!"

I just had a BOY SCOUT COCKTAIL--two of them and an old lady helps YOU across the street!

When I gave my kid a pony for his birthday, he said "What IS it, a FOREIGN HORSE?"

She's on a diet of cocoanuts and bananas. She hasn't lost any weight but Boy, can SHE climb TREES?

When people tell me I'm growing old, I remind them that I still chase pretty young girls. The only difference is now that I chase them I can't remember why I started CHASING them!

(NEXT PAGE)

laugh at HUNTLEY & BRINK..

I enjoy Las Vegas because everybody out there gambles. One day I went into a drug store for some aspirin and the Druggist said "I'll flip ya double or nothing!" I wound up with TWO HEADACHES!!

Her mother sings in a quartet. She's the BASS SINGER!

(NEXT PAGE)

ore a white dress.
ought she was a REFRIGERATOR!

She was too ugly to have her face lifted so they lowered her body instead!

(continued)

Cooper set a high standard, knew exactly what he was looking for and compiled a more compact A – Z index of his own. In fact, only a small percentage of what he highlighted as suitable corresponds to the material that became most associated with him down the years. Tommy always claimed that the hardest part of his television shows was pulling together his stand-up spots, which were mostly deemed his responsibility, as distinct from the sketches written by top comedy writers of the day and his mangled magic tricks, which to an extent chose themselves once he had been seduced by them in the heady atmosphere of the magic depots he loved frequenting. Needless to say, there was never a problem in having enough material in the end. Cooper may have thought he was subscribing to a joke service; but, in effect, the masses of paper that piled high in the Cooper home provided another service, acting as the lucky talisman against the day when his tried and tested stuff was taken away from him and audiences stopped laughing. The nightmare was an occupational hazard for any comic.

The exact pedigree of much of what Orben, Glason and the others purveyed is lost to history. Jokes often seem to be born without conception. We can recognise a joke as an old joke, but when we are honest with ourselves we are unlikely to have heard it before (unless it is an accepted favourite in an act like Cooper's, in which case we are disappointed when we don't hear it again) and are unable to pinpoint a source. But as Gershon Legman, the legendary chronicler of scatological humour, limericks, origami folds (sic) and much else besides, wrote, 'Nobody ever tells jokes for the first time.' The exaggeration contains a basic truth. Successful jokes are contagious and become modified in the passing and this has probably been so since the beginning of time.

At the very least Cooper stands as a colossus at a pivotal time in the oral tradition of jokes. He was indisputably the exemplar of the contagion process as applied to comedy. No British comic of recent times has been quoted by an adoring public more extensively for its own amusement than he has been, in a way that is tantamount to an extension of his own performance. Things also worked in reverse. Back in his early days jokes seemed to circulate far more freely amongst the profession, comics appropriating from one another with impunity, in a way that the more watchful ethos of the television and DVD era does not allow. A telling one-liner from the early part of his career went, *'Now get ready for this one – it's one of the first jokes I ever stole.'* When I asked Tommy's widow, Gwen – always known to him as 'Dove' – to identify for me the source of a particular piece of business he had featured in his act, she replied, 'I think we saw that in Vegas. We nicked it, like we nicked everything else!' Actually they didn't nick or steal anything, at least no more than anybody else, or Billy Glason.

Aside from the reams of purchased material that Tommy perused with dedicated attention, his quickly established reputation in British show business attracted comedy material from much nearer to home. His files overflow with submissions – mostly unsolicited – not only of jokes, but monologues, parodies, sketches, and comedy magic scenarios. Few ever saw the light of day on stage or screen. However, three names tower above the rest in any overview of his stand-up material and deserve recognition here. They are Val Andrews, Freddie Sadler, and Eddie Bayliss. Bayliss was a lorry driver by profession whose submissions fitted Cooper so magnificently that he was soon signed up by Tommy's agent to secure a hold on his services, although it does not appear that he ever totally gave up his day job. To Bayliss we owe, *'My feet are killing me – every night when I'm lying in bed they get me right round the throat like that'* and many other Cooper gems. Eddie also provided Tommy with one of his most precious visual comedy bits on the occasion of a Royal Gala before the Queen. Cooper took a sword from his table and with one eye on the Royal Box carefully laid it on the ground. He knelt expectantly behind it for a few telling seconds, during which nothing happened. Then he got up, reclaimed the weapon and shrugged, *'Well, you never know, do you?'* Even the Queen laughed.

Sadler's letterhead reveals that he was a 'Comedy Impressionist and Compère' on the London concert party circuit during the early fifties. His flair for one-liners was less spectacular than that of Bayliss, although fans should nod obeisance whenever they hear the line, *'Here we have a skipping rope – so we'll skip that!'* More importantly, amid many suggestions for misguided magic for Tommy's early television career, he co-devised with Val Andrews the single most memorable non-magical sequence in the performer's repertoire, the one with 'the Hats.' Val was a versatile individual who juggled the performing and selling of magic with comedy scriptwriting and the writing of Sherlock Holmes pastiches. Their joint creation, which began as an idea from Andrews and to the bones of which each subsequently added flesh, is immortalised in Cooper lore and while not a joke or series of jokes per se, calls out for inclusion in any book on Cooper's humour and will be found towards the end of these pages. It is doubtful if the pair ever received remuneration equal to the true worth of the routine and it is proper that Andrews and Sadler should be accorded proper credit here.

Whatever the source of his material, Cooper had an unerring ability to spot what would work for him. He once pinpointed what he was looking for when he explained that the two most important devices in comedy were a surprise and a funny picture. Unsurprisingly the following pages represent a surreal cartoon gallery of the unexpected: *'I slept like a log last night. I woke up in the fireplace.'* Most jokes are like magic tricks, deriving their energy from twists in logic or language or both, in the way that the art of conjuring takes liberties with the accepted realities of the world. A definitive Cooper gag has qualities of conciseness, and an outrageous courting of the obvious that might seem to contradict the surprise theory. However, Tommy, as a magician himself, knew that the most effective mysteries depended upon the simplest methods. However familiar audiences became with the outrageous literalism of so much of his wordplay, they never saw it coming, even when they had heard the joke several times before. It is appropriate that, as a man who with his bulk, grotesque features and jubilant raucousness embodied so many of the physical attributes of Mr Punch, he approached punch lines with an abandon that rendered the obvious momentarily invisible. Such is the misdirection of the great magician, as in, *'Sometimes I drink my whiskey neat. Other times I take my tie off and leave my shirt hanging out.'* Jerry Seinfeld has drawn a parallel between telling a joke and jumping over a metaphorical canyon with the audience coming along for the ride. No comic ever made the shortness of the gap more exhilarating than Cooper.

Freud famously said that jokes needed to convey their message not just in a few words, but in too few words. The manuscript records of his material that Cooper left behind reveal how he refined individual gags over the years, honing and polishing them to haiku-style intensity. Here Tommy is talking of his childhood early in his career:

I'll never forget the time I was doing a trick in the living room before an open fire – my father came home and almost killed me – we didn't have any fireplace!

This became:

One day I was doing tricks in front of a big fire. My father came in and hit me. We didn't have a fireplace!

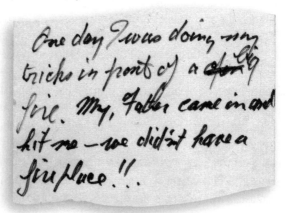

Sometimes one longer joke would in the course of time do more effective service as two. The topic is his wife:

One morning she got up with curlers in her hair, cream all over her face, wearing an old dressing gown and she went to take the rubbish out – and when she saw the rubbish lorry moving away, she said, 'Hey, am I too late?' and the dustman said, 'No, lady, jump in!'

This evolved into the double whammy of:

She ran after the dustman and said, 'Am I too late for the dustcart?' He said, 'No – jump in!'

alongside

She puts that cold cream on at night – curlers in her hair – then she puts a fishing net over the whole thing. She said, 'Kiss me.' I said, 'Take me to your leader!'

While Cooper became a past master when it came to brevity, his versatility set him out as an equal exponent of the honourable exception to all the rules, the device that takes perverse delight in delaying the resolution of the final punch line through any number of diversions and digressions. I refer to the shaggy dog story. Dogs seldom figure in them, although in Cooper's case other animals frequented them with amazing regularity. He had a habit of finding himself in the jungle so often that at the risk of paraphrasing Kipling one could refer to these escapades as his *Just Like That* stories, if not exactly his *Just So* ones. Several examples occur in the pages ahead. Cooper's strength was, of course, all in the telling. Where appropriate, I have interpolated his verbal asides and, as virtual stage directions, descriptions of the gestures and mannerisms that enabled him to bring these rambling and potentially boring discourses – together with much more – so hilariously to life.

It has been said of Cooper that many of his jokes could have come out of Christmas crackers. In fact, I have a favourite image of Tommy as Santa Claus, the capacious sack on his back spilling over with magic tricks and jokes – animal jokes, waiter jokes, dog jokes, doctor jokes, policeman jokes, wife jokes. The spirit of play underpinned his work in a childlike way, transporting his audience – temporarily released from the bonds of logic and reality – back to the euphoric state of childhood. Much of this world was the one of Dandy and Beano, although conversely many of his lines are suggestive of deeper philosophical reasoning, poised between ignorance and a more exalted mental power: *'Somebody once said that horsepower was a very good thing when only horses had it.'* One recalls his apparently simplistic statement that while other people paint apples, bananas and oranges, he paints the juice. As I said in *Always Leave Them Laughing*, my earlier biography of the comedian, such comments acknowledge 'a questioning of the way the world works that gets close to the higher level of conceptual or representational humour exploited so successfully by Spike Milligan in *The Goon Show*, going beneath the level of language to the fundamental structures of thought and life itself.' The frequency with which dream jokes recur in his repertoire is significant here: *'The other night I dreamt I was eating a ten-pound marshmallow. When I woke up the pillow had gone!'* Freud again likened jokes to dreams arguing that in both a topsy-turvy logic holds sway. Cooper was the funniest advocate of the theory. It was a bonus that even at the peak of his form and his physical condition no comedian conveyed a greater impression of sleepwalking through his act.

'WEE WILLIE WINKIE RUNS THROUGH THE TOWN UPSTAIRS AND DOWNSTAIRS IN HIS NIGHTGOWN... ...AND YOU THINK I'M NUTS!'

With Cooper nothing could be taken for granted. Even if the hilarity and festive ambience of his act imparted a safe feeling to his audiences, he could hit a disconcertingly macabre streak. A radio discussion programme once targeted a Tommy Cooper joke as the all-time greatest gag: *'This fellow knocked at a door and said, 'Hello – is Charlie in?' The woman replied, 'Charlie died last night.' The man said, 'He didn't say anything about a pot of paint, did he?'* Whether you find that funny or not – and it has to be admitted that it is closer to Gary Larson's *The Far Side* and *The Addams Family* than the typical Cooper joke – it sums up the futility of life itself, the human condition at literally its most skeletal. Steven Wright, the brilliantly dour American stand-up comedian who has done more than anyone to make existentialism an easy bedfellow of laughter, on one occasion analysed his own humour as 'the thoughts of a child, with an adult voice.' In my career as a television producer I once had the privilege of presenting Wright and Cooper as guests on the same show. Wright came out with lines like, 'Lots of comedians have people they try to mimic. I mimic my shadow' and 'He asked me if I knew what time it was. I said, "Yes, but not right now."' Their mutual respect upon discovering each other was joyous and I wish I could have signed up the visitor to write exclusively for Cooper there and then.

If Tommy knew what he was looking for, he also had self-imposed guidelines on what to avoid. Straightforward insult humour seemed reserved almost totally for his agent, Miff Ferrie, with whom his love-hate relationship has become an established part of recent British show business folklore. As for xenophobia, long a staple of the traditional stand-up, Tommy's joke about the Chinese Jews is purely a linguistic trick and is hostile to no one, while the joke about the Mexican, the Irishman and the German is as innocuous as the one about the three bears and relies as much on its three-part structure as on any latent racism for its humour. He hardly ever went further than that, unless it was the occasion at a Variety Club luncheon in honour of Dean Martin, when he addressed the crowd, 'When you think of Martin and Lewis, it's amazing how things have turned out. Dean Martin has become an international star known all over the world. I often wonder what happened to the Eyetie who did all the singing!' But Tommy had little time for stereotypes. When he wanted to joke about stupidity, he had only to direct the laugh against himself for the biggest response – apart, that is, from his long-suffering wife.

The tradition of the wife joke in the Cooper canon owes as much to his reverence for his boyhood comic hero, Max Miller, as for any aggression towards his partner in marriage, Gwen, for whom, in spite of what the tabloids have voiced to his apparent discredit in the years since his death, he maintained a deep-rooted love to the end of his days. This is not the place for an analysis of the complex emotional triangle of his latter years. The only relevant aspect of their relationship in our context is the advice Gwen, or 'Dove', gave him in his early days, namely that if he ever told a dirty joke on stage, she would divorce him. He more or less kept to that promise, and is on record as saying, 'Once you tell the first dirty joke you tell another and before you know where you are, you've got a blue show and I don't want that. It's very difficult to get back from blue material to clean material.' The nearest he got to the knuckle was on the back of a playground naughtiness, as in the prop gag with the three-cup brassiere – *'I met a funny girl last night!'* – although in scrutinising his comedy files it was perhaps surprising to find that he was not averse to the occasional one-liner that was more risqué – and even in today's climate more politically incorrect – than one obviously associates with him. For the record a selection of them is included here, but essentially you could guarantee the whiteness of your weekly wash by the standard set by Cooper's humour. And as for him taking lines from Maxie like *'I've got the best wife in England. The other one's in Africa!'* Gwen would have no qualms. There wasn't a woman who didn't adore the self-proclaimed Cheekie Chappie in his outrageous plus-fours and technicolour clothes, in spite of any insinuation that he might have been otherwise sexually disposed: 'Well, what if I am?'

In the joke appropriation stakes, no British comic was probably more sinned against than the great Max Miller. Max reigned triumphant as the 22-carat doyen of risqué humour throughout the thirties and the forties, Tommy's formative years. But he was never unsubtle and skilfully left the meaning of what he was saying to the imagination of his audience. Not only Cooper, but every member of his generation keen to ply the trade of comedian on the boards, wanted to emulate him, in awe not only of his daring and bravado, but his timing and technique. In the latter years of the great comedian's life, the young magician befriended his hero, whom he came to regard as a veritable guardian angel. Although he had no intention of discarding his fez, Tommy treasured Max's trademark white snap-brim trilby, which Miller presented to him. Their verbal styles were totally dissimilar – the one the shrill salty cadences of Brighton's seafront, the other the heavier burr of the West Country – and the full measure of how much Tommy appropriated from the older man's repertoire only became apparent to this writer when I confronted Tommy's notes of the material in question. Although both their repertoires were well known to me, I had not previously acknowledged the duplication, so distinctive had been their two deliveries. But while Tommy may have reworked material first popularised by his mentor, what he more importantly acquired from Max was the special creativity that goes into delivery and interpretation. Tommy's true copyright was in the rhythm and phrasing that all his impersonators have imitated, but which no one can steal in such a way as to claim as their own. It is all about discovering your own voice. Like Miller's, Tommy's delivery, with its emphases and skilled use of repetition, achieved an innate precision – unconscious maybe – that wholly belied the fumbling exterior of the dysfunctional magician.

It is seldom that Cooper comes in for criticism. When he does so, it is often down to the supposed antiquity of his material and his propensity for laughing at his own jokes. With regard to the former, he had no qualms. It all came back to self-belief. He once discussed telling the corniest joke in the world: 'You have to have such innocent faith in it that the audience just has to laugh.' Once Cooper had convinced himself that something was funny, the audience was already halfway to laughter. Billy Glason hit the nail on the head in his sales pitch: 'There are no old gags! The only thing old about old gags are the ones who've heard them before and the answer to those who want to admit their age when they remark that a gag is old, is "Say, you don't look that old!"' Tommy voiced his own feelings on the matter to his fellow magician, David Hemingway: 'It doesn't matter how old the gag is.

It doesn't matter how many times the audience has heard it before. If it's funny, it's funny.' And he was always the professional optimist. It may be that one of the fundamental rules of comedy is not to laugh at one's own jokes. But all rules are set to be broken and nothing enhanced the jokes he was telling more effectively than the distinctive foghorn-cum-chortle of a laugh that resonated at those key moments when he paced his material for maximum effect. There was the added advantage that as a character device it could register fear, nervousness, jubilation or act as supposed cover-up for his own inadequacy. Never did he overuse or misjudge the device. With it he could ride his audience like a surfer rides the waves.

Compiling this book has been helped by the vast accumulation of manuscript material Tommy left behind. He was completely methodical in his madness. When it came to props and magic tricks he never left a single thing to chance, making sure that he had two, sometimes three of everything he needed. Similarly, he seldom performed a show without the security of a cue sheet of tricks and gags sneaked away somewhere amongst the props that overburdened his table. Similarly he wrote out new material in long-hand as a means of fixing the joke and its rhythms in his mind. These cards may occasionally have found their way onto his table top too, although I defy anyone to recall a performance when he would have read from them slavishly. If stacked in a pile the amount of cardboard he used up in the process during his career must have come close to rivalling Nelson's Column. In a pre-recycling age, every single scrap of the material laying waste in the Cooper household was called into service. The sheets of cardboard that came to strengthen new shirts were particularly favoured: there were so many that one wonders if he ever wore the same shirt twice. Postcards, menu cards, even the slim cards that many moons ago were used to separate Shredded Wheat in the box were all called into play. By extracting much of this material from the cards themselves and reproducing it in facsimile, this book attempts to bring the reader closer to Cooper as he set out on the laughter trail.

The first prize will be a free extraction of a tooth
... own choice!!

... I had a polaroid camera so
... I could get a close up of that 300lbs. of putty for each member of ...
... dying ... those — Almost new!

And before I go lets have a
nice big hand for the boys in
the Forces.

I've had some wonderful evenings
and this isn't one of them.

Took my wife to the beach
I let her bury me in sand
then I buried her in sand
Next Summer I'm going to dig her

Hotel – 3 o'clock in morning
– Man loses his temper —
on door — What did you
Nothing. I just kept
my dimes

I'd like to say something
but I don't like
the spell.

He was but a
CAP + WRENCH
Who married a
LADY'S HAT with
He met her by ...

Audience Lines

... laugh I feel better than I look
... nervous tonight I'm afraid I'll
... funny.

... in a hurry don't worry I've got
... you get a dance

Quick Start Stories
... to send the wife to Scotland this summer
I'm marking time killing myself!

Did you enjoy the ride? Yes Man, ...
... the most poisonous, the

Text Man: I'll take the kids for nothing.

quiet like
for hours.

... Auntie
LADIES HA...
... she cou...

RING
... make you ...
AP + WRENCH
He was h...
Who spen...

TENNIS RAC...
Whilst th...
He got a...
And whe...

WALK W...
CLOTH ...
He sta...

Random Bits
... my wife is carry
... ns and she
... ed some thing different.
... he went to a furrier
... ssed a mink with
... lla. She got a
... coat, only the
... leaves are too long.

Gypsy fortune teller, who
doesn't read the tea leaves
She reads the lemon..

Bill Bailey. He's not com...

T.V.

and I wish you could
I've just come back
from H. wood — I made
two pictures, and there
One like this — the other
like that!! I'm proud of

I invite you a
chance to lau...

POST CARD

Opening! — Good
to me evening!

Health card, I you
I'll tell you.
aren't you going to
enter in for the social

Doctor)
Last night I looked up an old fri...
what a terrible sight!!
I spent an hour on the phone ...
... last night the settee would...

Any entertainer only succeeds because he or she corresponds to a particular moment in time and, although Cooper was not a topical or satirical comic who spun comedy out of the day's headlines, no attempt has been made in these pages to lose cultural references that may no longer carry the meaning they once did. Timothy Whites, Danish Bacon and Lux soap flakes, dairy queens, home perms and living bras need no other explanation than that they placard the era of his greatest success, even if it is hard to accept – as one joke inherited from Max Miller insists – that there was a time when Chelsea played in the 'second division' and that Cooper began his career when the future of television was less a foregone conclusion than one might have presumed: *'Everybody's saying television is here to stay. I don't know. The Hire Purchase company is taking mine back tomorrow.'* One line not included is the one he often resorted to when he had to pour water in a glass in the cause of a trick. Casting a wary glance at the liquid, he would muse, *'It'll never sell!'* long before the craze for bottled water became a licence for money to flow. One wonders what he would have made of the joke potential lurking within the minutiae of life today. It is not hard to hear him complaining that he couldn't get on the tube because his Oyster wouldn't open and that a Blackberry is a messy way to make a phone call, that the Amazon is a long way to go to buy a book and that he couldn't watch BBC because the Sky's the limit.

Hopefully his fans will derive enjoyment from the following pages and those who missed Tommy in his own lifetime will nevertheless have assimilated from reruns and tribute programmes enough about his voice, physical presence and persona to be able to read the contents with him in mind. I do not expect any reader to burst into laughter at seeing a joke reproduced in the cold context of print on the page, but I do beg people as they read to imagine the laughter that greeted Cooper as he performed it all, whether one-liner, shaggy dog tale, or the more continuous pieces where he was able to edit jokes together in such a way as to achieve a genuine conversational rapport with his audience. Let us not forget that Tommy's very best joke was the man himself, capable of making audiences laugh at the mere mention of his name. That presence informed his words in a mysterious alchemical way that even he never understood. He took jokes very seriously indeed, but I am equally sure that he would not have wanted this book to be taken too seriously.

'LADIES AND GENTLEMEN, TOMMY COOPER...'

(Tommy enters at start of his act to wild applause)
Thank you very much. Thank you. Now I must say you've been a wonderful audience and now I'm gonna finish with a little song. A little song entitled, 'I can't get over a girl like you, so get out of bed and make the tea yourself.'

You know I can always tell whether an audience is going to be good or bad. *(Sniffs)* Good night!!

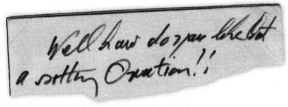

Well how do you like that – a sitting ovation!

I'm so nervous tonight, I'm afraid I'll say something funny.

You think I'm crazy – and you paid to come in!!

What happened? Somebody else come on?

What a lovely audience – I'll do the full act tonight – I won't cut a thing...

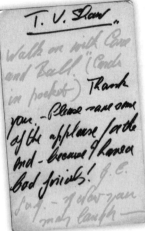

Thank you. Please save some of the applause for the end – because I have a bad finish!

I don't care what you think. I'm staying in show business!

If you think this weather has ruined your evening, wait until you see my act.

Do you know, I'd give anything to sit out there and watch this!

I have a bit of advice for hungry young comedians – eat something.

I spent three years learning judo – I had to – with an act like mine I had to defend myself!

I haven't been on TV for a while due to ill health. I make people sick!!

There was one man in one night. I said, 'Where are you going?' He said, 'I'm leaving.' I said, I'll come with you. I don't want to be on my own.'

I got a letter from my fan club. It said, 'Our membership is swelling. They've all got the mumps!'

Excuse me laughing – you all look so funny out there. You probably all think, what am I gonna do next. I don't know 'what I'm gonna do next.' I really don't!

They told me to have humility and be humble. I've never seen such a humiliating audience in my whole life!

Don't laugh – I feel better than I look.

TOMMY'S CHILDHOOD

Tommy was born on 19 March 1921 in Caerphilly in Wales. When he was three his family relocated to Exeter, where they remained until they moved again to Langley, just outside Southampton, when he reached his teens.

I was born at a very early age – I cried just like a baby.

I was a surprise to my parents. They found me on the doorstep. They were expecting a bottle of milk.

When I was a kid I had the cutest little button nose. But they couldn't feed me – it was buttoned to my lower lip.

My first day at school – I was so excited I cut myself shaving.

Then I grew up! I had to – what other way could I grow?

One day I was doing my tricks in front of a big fire. My father came in and hit me. We didn't have a fireplace!

When I was four years old my father caught me smoking. I'll never forget how he yelled at the kid who set me on fire.

I never had a present for Xmas! My father was a farmer and he use to go outside and fire his gun — and come in and say — Santa Clause has just committed suicide!!

I never had a present for Christmas! My father was a farmer and he used to go outside and fire his gun and come in and say, 'Santa Claus has just committed suicide.'

When the nurse said 'You've got an 8lb bundle of joy — She said 'Thank God the laundry's back.

When the nurse told my mother that we had an eight pound bundle of joy, my mother said, 'Thank god – the laundry's back.'

I was born with a silver knife in my mouth. My father was a sword swallower!

I was born with a silver knife in my mouth. My father was a sword swallower!

I was born with a silver spoon in my mouth. When they took it out I was alright.

Even when I was a kid I was always smiling. I swallowed a banana – sideways!

> *Jokes etc*
>
> *I was born with a silver spoon in my mouth – when they took it out I was alright.*

When I was born they thought I was going to be a footballer – because I dribbled on my bib!

> *when I was 2 years old I memorised the entire encyclopedia, but no one believed me because I couldn't talk!*

When I was two years old I memorised the entire Encyclopaedia Britannica, but no one believed me because I couldn't talk!

I shall never forget my father said to me, 'If you go into show business and disgrace the family, I shall disown you. I won't leave you any money at all.' And I said, 'I don't care, dada.' I did. 'Dada!' So he tried to bribe me. He bought me yachts, motorcars, aeroplanes, a gold studded yoyo, and I said, 'Dada.' I said, 'I don't want material things. I want love and affection. Get me a blonde!'

TOMMY'S
LAUGHTER
PRESCRIPTION

DOES MY VOICE SOUND A BIT HOARSE? IT DOES A BIT,
DOESN'T IT? TODAY I LOST MY VOICE – AND THE ONE I'M
USING NOW I BORROWED SPECIALLY FOR THE SHOW.

SERIOUSLY THOUGH I DID GO TO THE DOCTOR TODAY AND
HE SAID, 'OPEN YOUR MOUTH' AND HE SAID, 'A LITTLE RAW'
– JUST LIKE THAT – SO I WENT 'GRRRR...' NOT LOUD.
JUST 'GRRRR...' (SOFTLY)

AND HE SAID TO ME, 'WHILE YOU'RE HERE I'LL TEST YOUR
EARS, BECAUSE WHEN YOUR VOICE GOES IT AFFECTS THE
HEARING.' I SAID, 'RIGHT' AND HE SAID, 'WHAT I'M GOING
TO DO IS THIS. I WANT YOU TO GO OVER THERE, AND I'LL
GO OVER HERE, AND WHAT I'M GOING TO DO, I'M GOING TO
WHISPER SOMETHING TO YOU AND I WANT YOU TO REPEAT
IT.' I SAID, 'RIGHT.' SO HE WENT OVER THERE AND I WENT
OVER THERE AND HE SAID, 'HOW NOW, BROWN COW?' SO I
SAID, 'HOW NOW, BROWN COW?' HE SAID, 'PARDON?'

SO I SAID TO THE DOCTOR, 'HOW DO I STAND?'
HE SAID, 'THAT'S WHAT PUZZLES ME.'

I SAID, 'DOCTOR, I FEEL LIKE A PAIR OF CURTAINS.'
HE SAID, 'THEN PULL YOURSELF TOGETHER.'

'DOCTOR, DOCTOR,' I SAID, 'THERE'S SOMETHING WRONG
WITH MY FOOT. WHAT SHOULD I DO?' HE SAID, 'LIMP.'

THE DOCTOR SAID, 'YOU'RE IN SHOCKING SHAPE. DO YOU
DRINK HEAVILY?' I SAID, 'NO, BUT I'M WILLING TO LEARN.'

I SAID, 'CAN YOU GIVE ME SOMETHING FOR MY LIVER?'
HE GAVE ME A POUND OF ONIONS.

I THOUGHT I HAD INDIGESTION. THE DOCTOR SAID, 'WHAT
HAVE YOU BEEN EATING?' I SAID, 'OYSTERS.' THE DOCTOR
SAID, 'HOW DID THEY LOOK WHEN YOU OPENED THEM?'
I SAID, 'DO YOU HAVE TO OPEN THEM?'

THE DOCTOR ASKED ME IF I TOOK MY TEMPERATURE.
I SAID, 'NO. IS IT MISSING?'

I SAID, 'DOCTOR, CAN YOU GIVE ME SOME SLEEPING PILLS
FOR MY WIFE.' HE SAID, 'WHY?' I SAID, 'SHE WOKE UP!'

I SAID 'DOCTOR, I GET THESE TERRIBLE DREAMS.'
HE SAID, 'WHAT'S THAT?' AND I SAID, 'I KEEP DREAMING
THESE BEAUTIFUL GIRLS, THESE BEAUTIFUL GIRLS KEEP
COMING TOWARDS ME, KEEP COMING TOWARDS ME – I
KEEP PUSHING THEM AWAY – THESE BEAUTIFUL GIRLS KEEP
COMING TOWARDS ME AND I KEEP PUSHING THEM AWAY,
PUSHING THEM AWAY.' HE SAID, 'WHAT DO YOU WANT ME
TO DO?' I SAID, 'BREAK MY ARM!'

Sunday Show

1. Pillow in bed, laying this side & the other side. Wife rolled her hair gag. Door Bolted Gag.

2. Doctor, I'm losing all sense of direction — what shall I do? Get <u>lost</u>.

3. Old Lady across the street gag. into Ploughman's Lunch.

4. Finish now with a song:- "When you walk through the storm keep your head up high" — I did that & fell in a puddle!

5. Irishman looking in mirror gag.

I SAID, 'DOCTOR, I'M LOSING ALL SENSE OF DIRECTION.
WHAT SHOULD I DO?' HE SAID, 'GET LOST.'

TOMMY
AT THE SEASIDE

You know, I was in Margate last summer for the summer season. A friend of mine said you want to go to Margate – it's good for rheumatism. So I went and I got it. And I tried to get into a hotel – it was so packed. So I went to this big boarding house and I knocked at the door and the landlady put her head out of the window and said, 'What do you want?' I said, 'I wanna stay here.' She said, 'Well stay there,' and she shut the window. And while I was there I bought one of these skin diving outfits. Have you seen them? Like a frogman's suit. Bought the whole thing – goggles, flippers, tank on the back. And I had a photograph taken like that – and like that! You never know, do you? You never know. And I went to the pier and I jumped in, cos you're not supposed to dive in – it's dangerous. And I jumped in like that and I think I turned a little bit on the way down and I went down about a hundred and fifty feet. It was lovely – very quiet – and I'm going along like that. *(Makes swimming gesture with right arm, holding left hand out in front of him)* I've got the instructions here! And I get rid of them and start going out like that *(Mimes with other arm)* and the feet are going like that *(Makes flipper movement with hands)* – not in the front, in the back – do you know what I mean? And I don't care now. I'm all over the place – the goggles getting all misty – and I'm humming to myself – not loud – just zzzzzz *(Very low)* and all of a sudden I saw a man walking towards me in a sports jacket and grey flannels. I thought that's unusual for a Tuesday. So I went towards him – moving like this – and I got right up to him and I got this pad out and wrote on it, 'What are you doing down here walking about in a sports jacket and grey flannels?' And he took this pad from me and wrote on it, 'I'm drowning.'

TOMMY
AND HIS
DOG

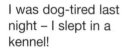

I was dog-tired last
night – I slept in a
kennel!

I've got a dog, you know.
I have. He's a one-man dog. He only bites me.

He took a chunk out of my leg the other day.
A friend of mine said, 'Have you put anything on it?'
I said, 'No, he liked it as it is.'

I'm only joking. He's harmless, really. But he's getting on a bit.
I said to him, 'Attack,' and he had one.

I just bought a watchdog and what do you think he watches? TV!

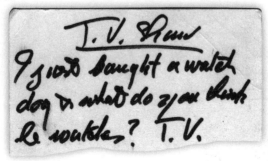

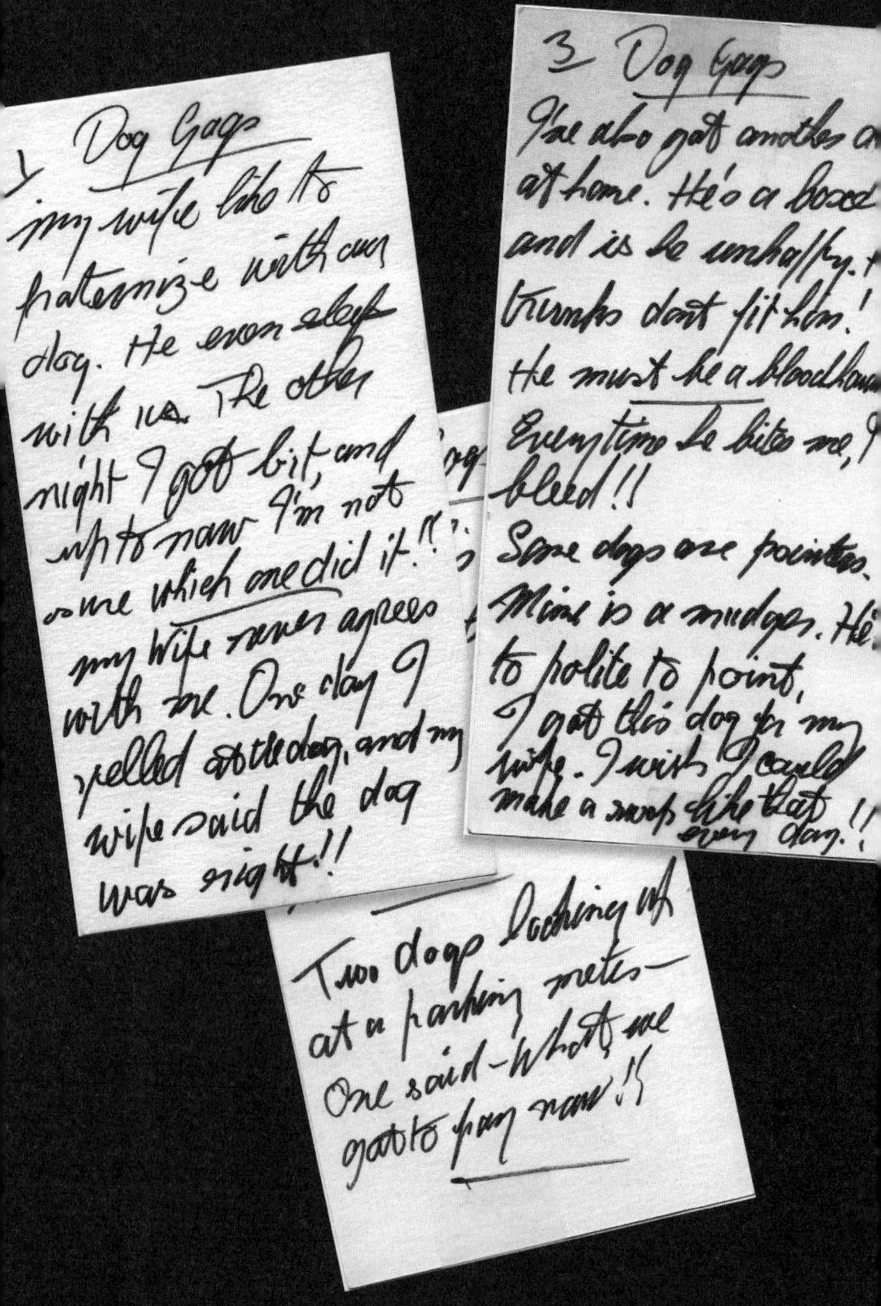

1 Dog Gags

my wife like to
fraternize with our
dog. He even sleep
with us. The other
night I got bit, and
up to now I'm not
sure which one did it!!
my wife never agrees
with me. One day I
yelled at the dog, and my
wife said the dog
was right!!

3 Dog Gags

I've also got another on
at home. He's a boxer
and is so unhappy. t
trunks don't fit him!
he must be a bloodhound
Every time he bites me, I
bleed!!
Some dogs are pointers.
Mine is a mudger. He's
to polite to point.
I got this dog for my
wife. I wish I could
make a swop like that
every day!!

Two dogs looking up
at a parking meter—
One said—What's we
got to pay now!?

My wife likes to fraternise with our dog. He even sleeps with us. The other night I got bit and up to now I'm not sure which one did it!

My wife never agrees with me. One day I yelled at the dog and my wife said the dog was right!

I've also got another dog at home. He's a boxer and is he unhappy! His trunks don't fit him.

He must be a bloodhound. Every time he bites me, I bleed!!

Some dogs are pointers. Mine is a nudger. He's too polite to point.

I got this dog for my wife. I wish I could make a swap like that every day!

Two dogs looking up at a parking meter – one said, 'What! We've got to pay now?'

I had a dog that was so silly he chased parked cars!!

I bought my girl a lapdog, but she got rid of it. Every time she sat on the dog's lap it bit her!

COOPER'S
LAUGHTER
ALLSORTS

THIS FELLOW KNOCKED AT A DOOR AND SAID, 'HELLO. IS CHARLIE IN?' THE WOMAN REPLIED, 'CHARLIE DIED LAST NIGHT.' THE MAN SAID, 'HE DIDN'T SAY ANYTHING ABOUT A POT OF PAINT, DID HE?'

HERE'S A QUICK JOKE. THERE'S A MAN, SEE, AND HE'S SITTING ON TOP OF A BUS AND HE'S GOT A BANANA STICKING OUT OF HIS EAR. A BANANA STICKING OUT OF HIS EAR! WELL, ANOTHER MAN SAW THIS, COS HE WAS WATCHING HIM LIKE THAT. AND HE SAID TO HIMSELF, 'WELL, I MUST TELL HIM.' WELL HE WOULD, WOULDN'T HE? SO HE WENT UP TO HIM AND HE SAID, 'EXCUSE ME.' AND THE MAN SAID, 'SPEAK UP. I'VE GOT A BANANA STICKING OUT OF MY EAR!'

WHAT A WONDERFUL DAY IT'S BEEN. DO YOU KNOW IT'S BEEN SEVENTY DEGREES IN THE SHADE. I WAS CLEVER. I STAYED IN THE SUN! ACTUALLY, I DID A LITTLE BIT OF SUNBATHING. I WAS LYING OUT THERE TODAY. A LITTLE BOY CREPT ACROSS AND POURED SOMETHING ALL OVER MY BACK. HE SAID, 'THIS'LL MAKE YOU BROWN.' I SAID, 'WHAT IS IT?' HE SAID, 'GRAVY!'

DID YOU HEAR THE JOKE – THERE WAS A FOREMAN ON A BUILDING SITE AND HE LOOKED TO THE MAN AT THE TOP OF THE LADDER AND HE SAID, 'YOU – GET YOUR MONEY AND YOUR CARDS. YOU'RE FINISHED.' HE SAID, 'EH?' HE SAID, 'GET YOUR MONEY AND YOUR CARDS. YOU'RE FINISHED.' HE SAID, 'EH?' HE SAID, 'FORGET IT. I'LL SACK SOMEBODY ELSE!'

TROOPER COOPER

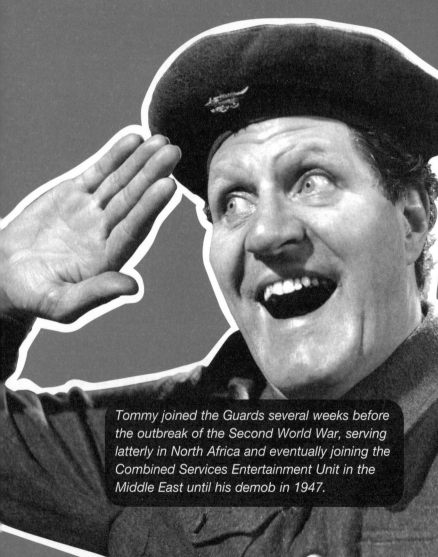

Tommy joined the Guards several weeks before the outbreak of the Second World War, serving latterly in North Africa and eventually joining the Combined Services Entertainment Unit in the Middle East until his demob in 1947.

Isn't it funny? Even in the army everything went wrong with me. It did really. I shall never forget when I first joined. They said to me, 'Would you like a commission?' I said, 'No – just a straight salary!'

There's this about the army – you never have to decide on what to wear. I just tried on my old army uniform and the only thing that fits is the tie.

There's this about the Army – you never have to decide on what to wear. I just tried on my old Army uniform and the only thing that fits is the tie.

When I was in the army my uniform fitted me like a glove. It covered my hand!

We had a sergeant and he used to call us out for roll call, you know, at four o'clock in the morning. Pitch black it was and he had a huge hurricane lamp in his hand and he used to say, 'Good morning, men' and we used to say, 'Good morning, lamp.' We couldn't see him!

And when you're on guard duty, they always teach you when you hear someone coming towards you in the dark to say with the rifle, 'Halt – who goes there – friend or foe?' You had to do that! 'Halt – who goes there – friend or foe?' *(Mimes drill)* Like that. And if they say 'Friend', you say 'Pass, friend.' Right. And I was on guard. I was on guard duty and it was very dark and I heard footsteps. 'Halt! Who goes there? Friend or foe?' And a voice said, 'Foe.' I said, 'How tall are you?' He said, 'Nine foot six.' I said, 'Pass, foe!'

I was seven years in the Horse Guards. It's like only yesterday. Now there's this sentry on guard duty and it's about four o'clock in the morning. It's very dark and he's got the rifle there *(Mimes accordingly)* and he's marching up and down and he's standing there about four o'clock in the morning and he falls asleep. Now that's a crime. I mean, they could put you inside for that straight away. So he's standing there asleep like that – he's standing there and all of a sudden the sergeant comes round the corner with the orderly officer. And now he's standing right in front of him. And there he is asleep *(Tommy looks dozy)* and there's the sergeant major like that *(Tommy looks fierce)*. And all of a sudden the sentry opens his eyes just a little bit like that – not much – just a little bit, and he can see them standing there. So he's gotta think now, hasn't he? He has, or otherwise he's gonna be inside. So he waits for a second and he's standing there and he opens his eyes like that and he says, 'Amen!' Huh, huh. It's lucky I wasn't court-martialled!

COOPER'S FEZ TALES

Everybody asks me where it came from. I'll tell you. I was in Egypt. In the army. Used to wear a pith helmet in the act in those days. A pith helmet, can you imagine? Not quite the same is it? Anyhow, one day I lost the bloody thing. Had to grab the first hat I could find. Then this waiter came by wearing one of these. That was that.

Then a few years ago I went back to Egypt with the wife. There was this guy selling fezzes in the market. I went to try one on and he turned to me and said, *'Just like that.'* I said, 'How do you know that? That's my catchphrase.' He said, 'Catchphrase? I know nothing about any catchphrase. All I know is that every time an English person tries one on, they turn to their friends and say, *"Just like that!"'* And then he said, 'You're the first one not to say it.' Priceless, isn't it?

TOMMY
IN THE JUNGLE

Now, here's a quick joke. What was it? Oh yes!

Did you hear the story of the king of the jungle? You know – the king of the jungle – the lion. And one day he woke up – he had a very bad temper – and he said to himself, 'I've just got to go outside now and teach them all who's the king of the jungle. Just to teach them.' So he gets up and he goes, 'Ooaarrhh!!' He was really mad. You know what I mean. 'Ooaarrhh!' And he saw a little chimp and he said, 'You! Who's the king of the jungle?' and he said, 'You, you're the king of the jungle.' 'Well that's alright then – alright.' And he walked along a bit more and he came across a laughing hyena and he said, 'Hey you, laughing boy.' And he went 'Hah hah hah hah hah! Hah hah hah hah hah!' He said, 'Who's the king of the jungle?' 'Ooh, hah hah hah! You are, you are.' So he walked on a little bit further and right at the very end was an elephant and a gorilla talking. And this gorilla looked at the elephant and he said, 'Here he comes, Jumbo. He's gonna do that king of the jungle bit again. He always does it.' He said, 'I'm not gonna stand it any more. I'm gonna leave you.' And he went up a tree. He said, 'I'll give you a trunk call later!' Hah hah hah! So the lion went up to this elephant and he said, 'Hey you!' He said, 'I'm talking to you big ears.' He said, 'Who's the king of the jungle?' And this elephant got his trunk and wrapped it right round him and threw him up in the air and as he was up in the air coming down he was going, 'Who's the king of the jungle? Who's the king of the jungle?' And he hit the ground hard and the elephant picked him up again and he threw him against the tree and he threw him against the other one. Then the other one and the other one! And the lion sank to the ground like that. It may have been like that. No, it was like that! And he said to the elephant, 'Look, there's no good getting mad just because you don't know the answer!'

HOMAGE TO MAX MILLER

The pre-eminent stand-up comedian of his era, Max Miller was the inspiration for a whole new generation of British comedians, not least Tommy Cooper. His sparkling personality and brilliant technique rightly earned him the label of 'The Pure Gold of the Music Hall.'

I've got the best wife in England. The other one's in Africa. 'Ere!'
The other day I came home and the wife was crying her eyes out.
I said, 'What are you crying for?' She said, 'I'm homesick.' I said, 'This is your home.' She said, 'I know. I'm sick of it!'

Here's a little rhyme now.

Adam and Eve
in the garden dwelt,
They were so happy
and jolly.
I wonder how they
would have felt
If all the leaves
had been holly!

(TOMMY PICKS UP ON INDIVIDUAL LAUGH OF WOMAN CACKLING IN THE CROWD)

I KNEW YOU WERE IN, BUT DIDN'T KNOW WHERE YOU WERE SITTING!

SO I SAID TO THIS LADY, I SAID, 'ARE YOU FAMILIAR WITH SHAKESPEARE?' SHE SAID, 'AS A MATTER OF FACT I AM. I HAD DINNER WITH HIM LAST NIGHT.' I SAID, 'WHAT ARE YOU TALKING ABOUT? HE'S BEEN DEAD FOR YEARS.' SHE SAID, 'I THOUGHT HE WAS QUIET.' 'ERE!'

THERE'S A LADY OVER THERE GOT OPERA GLASSES ON ME. SHE THINKS I'M A RACEHORSE!

My wife came in the other day and she said, 'What's different about me?' And I said, 'I don't know - what is different about you? Have you had your hair done?' She said, 'No.' I said, 'Have you got a new dress on?' She said, 'No.' I said, 'Have you got a new pair of shoes?' She said, 'No.' I said. 'Well what is it? What's different?' She said, 'I'm wearing a gas mask.'

There's a man won the football pools, see, and he said to himself, 'I'll buy a car.' So he went down to the salesroom and saw the salesman and he said, 'I'd like a car. How much is that?' He said, 'Eight hundred pounds.' He said, 'I can't afford that. Eight hundred pounds? I only won seventy-five pounds.' 'Well,' the salesman said, 'How about a bicycle?' He said, 'I don't want a bike. I want to get out in the country to get some fresh air.' 'Well,' he said,

'how about a pair of skates?' He said, 'Get away! I want to get out. I don't want skates.' And the man said, 'I tell you what. How about a hoop and a stick?' He said, 'Alright.' So he bought a hoop and a stick and he went out into the country, came across a pub, and put the hoop and stick in the car park. He went inside, had a drink, came out and the stick's gone. Somebody's pinched it. So he went back to the landlord and said, 'Somebody's taken my stick. They've pinched it.' And the landlord said, 'Don't get excited. It can't have cost you much.' He said, 'Well, it only cost me half a crown, but that's not the point. How am I going to get home?'

MEET THE WIFE

Although her real name was Gwen, Tommy always referred to his wife as 'Dove.' They met while they were both performing for the troops soon after the Second World War and married in Nicosia on 24 February 1947. The marriage endured until the day he died.

HER BROTHER SAID TO ME, 'SHE SMOKES IN BED,'
AND I SAID 'WHAT'S THE MATTER WITH THAT,
LOTS OF PEOPLE SMOKE IN BED.'
AND HE SAID 'WHAT, FACE DOWN?'

Her brother said to me, "She smokes in bed," and
I said "Whats the matter with that, lots of people
smoke in bed," and he said "what? face down."

She said to me, "Do you mind if I wear my hair
in a bun," I said, I don't care if you wear it in
a loaf of bread."

SHE SAID TO ME, 'DO YOU MIND IF I WEAR MY HAIR
IN A BUN?'
I SAID, 'I DON'T CARE IF YOU WEAR YOUR HAIR IN A
LOAF OF BREAD.'

AND SHE'S ALWAYS ON A DIET, MY WIFE. ALWAYS ON A
DIET. SHE'S ON A DIET NOW. EATS NOTHING BUT COCONUTS
AND BANANAS ALL DAY LONG. COCONUTS AND BANANAS.
SHE HASN'T LOST ANY WEIGHT, BUT YOU SHOULD SEE HER
CLIMB TREES!

MY WIFE – SHE'S ALWAYS ON A DIET. SHE'S ON ONE NOW.
SHE DRINKS EIGHT GLASSES OF WATER A DAY.
SHE'S LOST EIGHT POUNDS AND GAINED FIFTY GALLONS.

MY WIFE WANTED HER FACE LIFTED. THEY COULDN'T DO IT,
SO FOR TWENTY POUNDS THEY LOWERED HER BODY.

THE WIFE. IT'S HER BIRTHDAY NEXT WEEK AND I NEVER KNOW WHAT TO GET HER. I DON'T KNOW WHETHER TO GET HER A BOX OF CHOCOLATES, A DIAMOND RING, A FUR COAT OR NEW CAR.
THAT'S WHAT I'LL GET HER – A BOX OF CHOCOLATES!

IN ACTUAL FACT MY WIFE JUST PHONED ME BEFORE THE SHOW.
SHE SAID, 'I'VE GOT WATER IN THE CARBURETTOR.'
I SAID, 'WHERE'S THE CAR?'
SHE SAID, 'IN THE RIVER.'

MY WIFE HAS STOOD BY MY SIDE EVER SINCE WE WERE MARRIED – BUT THEN WE HAVE ONLY ONE CHAIR IN THE HOUSE. OH DEAR!

MY WIFE USED TO SAY, 'I'D GO TO HELL AND BACK FOR YOU.'
I SAID, 'YOU DON'T HAVE TO COME BACK JUST FOR ME.'

MY WIFE SAID, 'YOU'LL DRIVE ME TO MY GRAVE.'
I HAD THE CAR OUT IN TEN MINUTES.

I'VE JUST GIVEN THE WIFE A JAGUAR. I HOPE IT TEARS HER TO PIECES.

SHE WAS LOOKING AT A WOMAN'S MAGAZINE AND SHE SAW THIS FUR COAT.
SHE SAID, 'I WANT THAT.' SO I CUT IT OUT AND GAVE IT TO HER.

I GOT A NEW CAR FOR THE WIFE YESTERDAY – NOT A BAD SWAP!

THAT FACE OF HERS! WHEN SHE SUCKS A LEMON,
THE LEMON PULLS A FACE.

SHE SAID, 'THE STOVE HAS GONE OUT.' I SAID, 'LIGHT IT.'
SHE SAID, 'I CAN'T. IT'S GONE OUT THROUGH THE CEILING.'

SHE UNDERCOOKS EVERYTHING. WE HAD OXTAIL SOUP THE
OTHER NIGHT AND THE TAIL WAS STILL WAGGING!

WHEN SHE COOKS YOU GET A LUMP IN YOUR THROAT –
IN YOUR STOMACH – YOUR ARMS – YOUR LEGS.

ALL SHE WANTED TO DO
WAS EAT OUT. SO WE
ATE OUT IN THE GARAGE!

MY WIFE WAS IN THE
BEAUTY SHOP TWO
HOURS. THAT WAS JUST
FOR THE ESTIMATE!

DO YOU WANT
TO DRIVE YOUR
WIFE CRAZY?
WHEN YOU GO TO
BED, DON'T TALK
IN YOUR SLEEP.
JUST GRIN.

I LIKE THE WAY SHE
HOLDS HER HEAD –
UNDER HER ARM!

My wife was in
the beauty shop two
hours. That was just
for the estimate!!
Do you want to drive
your wife crazy? When
you go to bed dont
talk in your sleep.
Just grin!!

I DID HER PORTRAIT IN OILS.
SHE HAS A FACE LIKE A SARDINE!

I FOUND A WAY TO CURE MY WIFE OF FALLING OUT OF BED.
I MAKE HER SLEEP ON THE FLOOR.

I PROMISED HER A MINK FOR HER BIRTHDAY ON ONE
CONDITION – SHE HAD TO KEEP HIS CAGE CLEAN!

A LORRY CAME ALONG AND KNOCKED HER DOWN AND I
SAID TO THE DRIVER, 'WHAT'S THE MATTER WITH YOU? WHY
DIDN'T YOU GO ROUND HER?'
HE SAID, 'I DIDN'T HAVE ENOUGH PETROL.'

SHE WORE HER MOTHER'S WEDDING DRESS.
IT WAS A BIT TIGHT – HER MOTHER WAS STILL IN IT!

You know I've been getting these terrible bad dreams. Terrible. The other night I dreamt I was eating a ten-pound marshmallow. When I woke up the pillow had gone!

Last night I dreamt I was plucking a chicken. Woke up the next morning and the wife was bald.

Some people sleep in pyjama trousers, and some people sleep in pyjama tops. Me? I just sleep in the string!

I slept like a baby last night – with my foot in my mouth!

These days you can't trust anybody. Last night I walked in my sleep and when I got back someone had walked off with my mattress.

Boy, am I tired! I was up half the night trying to remember something I wanted to do. Then it dawned on me – I planned to go to bed early!

If you've got insomnia, don't lose any sleep over it!

They've got a new cure for insomnia – a pill that weighs 200 pounds. You don't swallow it – you drop it on your head.

I couldn't sleep last night so I got up at three a.m. and made tea in my pyjamas. I couldn't find the teapot anywhere!

They gave me a lovely dressing room – all made of tile with 14 taps!!

If you've got insomnia – don't lose any sleep over it!

They've got a new cure for insomnia, a pill that weighs 200lbs. You don't swallow it, you drop it on your head!!

He was so bow-legged his wife swung him over the door for good luck!

I couldn't sleep last night got up 3AM, & made tea in my pyjamas I couldn't find the teapot anywhere!! –

I feel good tonight. I was up at the crack of six this morning. Took a brisk walk to the bathroom and was back in bed at five past six.

TOMMY'S
ONE-LINERS

Did you see me pick that up? I'm not afraid of work!

I went to a plastic surgeon – he looked almost real.

I missed my catnap today – I slept right through it.

I played golf the other day – got a hole in one – the other sock was perfect.

I feel good tonight. There's nothing like a cold bath – full of hot water!

I've got acting in my blood – many years ago a straight actor bit me!

I'm so near-sighted I can't even see my contact lenses.

I was just thinking – what do you give to a sick florist?

She was bowlegged, he was knock-kneed – when they stood together they spelled OX!

Have you ever been to an Eskimo wedding? They blow out the cake and eat the candles.

I went in a pub and had a ploughman's lunch – he wasn't half mad!

I've tiptoed into my house so often at 4 a.m. in the morning, my neighbours think I'm a ballet dancer.

I went golfing the other day. I dug up so many worms, I decided to go fishing!

Now here's a quick laugh. Do this tomorrow. Go into an antique shop and say 'What's new?'

They always say take an aspirin for a headache – who wants a headache?

Did you hear the joke about the fire eater? She hiccupped and cremated herself?

Did you hear about the Salvation Army drummer who quit because his mother didn't want him hanging around on street corners!

Did you hear about the Salvation Army drummer who quit because his mother didn't want him hanging around on street corners!

I was a dancer once. I was. I did Swan Lake. I fell in.

I said 'I'd like a cornet, please.' She said, 'Hundreds and thousands?' I said 'No. One will do me very nicely.'

TOMMY ON STAGE

Here's a little trick for you now.
In fact it's a matter of life and death.
I shall now attempt to throw these three
cards into that hat there, so I'd like a drum
roll please.
*(Stands back at a distance and scales first
card in direction of the hat...)*
Missed! *(Repeats with second card...)*
Missed!
Now if I miss this time,
I'm going to shoot
myself. *(Repeats
with third card and
misses again...)*
Missed!
*(Goes to table,
picks up gun in
exasperation,
goes into
wings,
a gunshot is
heard, then after
the briefest of pauses
Tommy walks back...)*
Missed!
Huh huh huh!

> *Phone in piano – (Ring: Voice –*
> *Is dat T. C. T. Yes. – V. Well I'd like*
> *to ask you something. T. Not now. I'm*
> *in a middle of a show. Voice. – What show*
> *are you watching?!! You must be nuts.*
> *Voice'. – You think I'm nuts – who ever*
> *heard of anyone keeping a phone inside*
> *a piano.!!!*

(Half-way through his act the phone rings in the piano – Tommy picks up the receiver)

Voice: Is that Tommy Cooper?

Tommy: Yes.

Voice: Well, I'd like to ask you something.

Tommy: Not now – I'm in the middle of a show.

Voice: What show are you watching?

Tommy: You must be nuts.

Voice: You think I'm nuts! Whoever heard of anyone keeping a phone inside a piano.

And now, ladies and gentlemen, this trick I'm gonna show you now is pretty dangerous. I could break my neck doing this ...

(Tommy takes off his jacket and draws attention to two chairs balanced precariously on a small table which has been brought on stage by two stagehands...)

...so, if I meet with an accident, I'd like to take my applause now.

(Tommy beckons audience to applaud...)

I'm not gonna break my neck for that!

(Tommy puts jacket back on, dismisses stagehands, who remove the furniture, and nothing more is said of the matter!)

TOMMY AND HIS AGENT

MIFF FERRIE

ENTERTAINMENTS

(INCORPORATING MIFF FERRIE ORCHESTRAS)

TEL. (01) 235 9854

GRAMS ENMIFF, LONDON, S.W.1

CABLES

Artiste's Name .... Tommy Cooper

It is understood that Miff Ferrie Entertainments act only as Agent and is in no w...

of Contract on the part of either the Proprietor or Artiste through whatever ...

To MIFF FERRIE ENTERTAINMENTS

IN CO...

hereby agree to a...

Television

appear ...

t "LIVE...

at...

at...

at...

Tommy's love-hate relationship with his agent and manager became legendary in show business circles. In the thirties Miff Ferrie had himself been famous as the leader of the Jackdauz, a popular music combination of the day.

MIFF FERRIE'S JAKDAUZ

I've got a clause in my contract that says I have to be cremated – so that my agent can get ten per cent of my ashes!

He's only dull and uninteresting until you get to know him. After that he stinks!

He's so crooked he has to screw on his socks!

If he offers you a deal, see a lawyer. And if the lawyer approves, see a second lawyer.

Success never changed him. He's still the same arrogant swine he was when he was a failure!

He said, 'Here's a cheque for your trouble.' I said, 'I haven't had any trouble.' He said, 'Wait until you cash that cheque!'

TOMMY GOES DOWN MEMORY LANE

Some of the places I played in the early days! I was doing the act at this club one night. They were throwing bread rolls at me and trying to knock my fez off and I was scared out of my mind – these were the hard men of London out there – and I didn't know what to do, so I just said, 'Stop that!' I don't know what possessed me. But I had to say something. The place came over funny. 'Stop what?' shouted this geezer. I said, 'Why, stop throwing all these bread rolls and that.' 'And why should I stop?' he shouted back. 'Well, because I haven't got an ad-lib for people throwing bread rolls at me.' The place fell about. It was never quite so hard after that, but you're never completely home and dry.

COOPER'S HECKLER STOPPERS

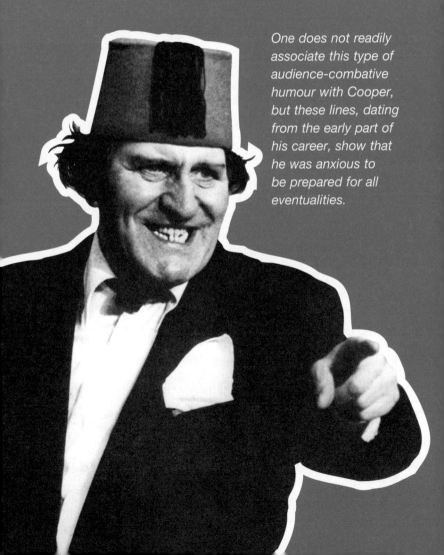

One does not readily associate this type of audience-combative humour with Cooper, but these lines, dating from the early part of his career, show that he was anxious to be prepared for all eventualities.

Heckler — S.toppers

The last time I saw a head like
that a jockey was bending over it

If anyone puts a price on your head
— take it.

He can't match wits wid me —
I haven't got any wits to match
him with.

It's just lucky for you that I'm a
scholar, a gentleman and a coward.

How would you like to come out
to my car and smell the exhaust
pipe?

Good for you. You made
a joke. What are you trying to
do — top your parents?)

The last time I saw a head like that a jockey was bending over it.

If anyone puts a price on your head – take it.

He can't match wits with me – I haven't got any wits to match him with.

It's just lucky for you that I'm a scholar, a gentleman and a coward.

How would you like to come out to my car and smell the exhaust pipe?

Good for you – you made a joke. What are you trying to do – top your parents?

You're laughing now – wait until you see the cheque.

What's the matter – did you get up on the wrong side of the floor this morning?

Don't mind them – they're left over from last night.

(Of a blousy female) The bride of Frankenstein! Most people have bags under their eyes! She's got bags over her eyes.

She's got a face that looks like it wore out six bodies.

Anybody's got the right to be ugly, but you abuse the privilege.

The way he's nursing that scotch and soda, you'd think he was drinking from an hour glass.

I never forget a face, but in your case I'll make an exception.

His head is so big, he can't get a headache to fit him.

TOMMY'S EARLY
STAND-UP

OPENING OF SHOW

Excuse me, sir. Have you seen a tall good-looking man in evening dress wearing a fez – I'm lost!!! Just call me razor blade – I'm sharp tonight!

Do you know the funniest thing happened to me coming here tonight. I wish I could remember what it was. It's not funny, but it takes up time.

By the way, how do you like my new suit? Do you think the style will ever come back?

Fits well. This is not my stomach – I've just got a low chest!

I was told it was a special show tonight – so I'm wearing tails.

(Tommy reaches down and produces a couple of actual fox tails)

Please! Please! The other acts'll think it's a fix – and they'd be right.

You're such a lovely audience – you deserve me!

What a reception! Who did the warm-up? Bob Hope?

Everybody's saying television is here to stay. I don't know. The Hire Purchase company is taking mine back tomorrow.

I was at a show last week. They said money was no object, so they didn't give me any.

I've been ill. Yes, I was in bed with 104 – and let me tell you, that's a lot of people in one bed.

Please relax. Just treat me as the interval.

I'm sorry I'm a bit late, but I had to pour water over my smoking jacket.

I've been waiting so long I forgot my act.

I've been lying low for months – my bed sags. I'm not myself. What can you expect of a day that begins with getting up?

Two psychiatrists pass each other on the street. One says, 'Hello.' The other says, 'I wonder what he meant by that.'

Keep it up. Flattery will get you somewhere. I started here six months ago and it seems only yesterday, and you know what a lousy day yesterday was.

COOPER'S
PUB TALES

Ye Olde
Fez & Tassel

I WAS OUT IN THE PUB HAVING A DRINK JUST BEFORE THE SHOW AND I WAS STANDING THERE AND I FELT A HAND GOING INTO MY POCKET. A HAND. SO I LOOKED ROUND AND I SAW THIS MAN STANDING THERE WITH HIS HAND AND I SAID, 'WHAT ARE YOU DOING?' HE SAID, 'I'M LOOKING FOR A MATCH.' I SAID, 'WHY DIDN'T YOU ASK ME?' HE SAID, 'I DON'T TALK TO STRANGERS.'

I WENT ON A DRINKING MAN'S DIET. YOU JUST DRINK AND DRINK AND DRINK UNTIL YOU FALL OVER. HOW DO YOU LOSE WEIGHT? TRYING TO GET UP!

A BIG WHITE HORSE WALKS INTO A PUB. THE BARMAN SAID, 'WE HAVE A DRINK NAMED AFTER YOU.'
THE HORSE SAID, 'WHAT? ERIC?'

A TRAMP WALKED INTO A PUB AND YELLED, 'WHAT'S THE MATTER WITH EVERYBODY? NOBODY'S GOT WHAT I WANT!' 'WHAT DO YOU WANT?' ASKED THE BARMAN AND THE TRAMP SAID, 'CREDIT!'

A DRUNK DROVE HIS CAR ALL THE WAY DOWN FROM MANCHESTER TO LONDON. THE POLICE ASKED HIM WHY HE DROVE DOWN IN THAT CONDITION. HE SAID, 'THEY WOULDN'T LET ME ON THE PLANE LIKE THIS!'

A DRUNK STAGGERED OUT OF A PUB AND JUST MADE IT TO THE PARKING METER. HE PUT A SIXPENCE IN THE METER AND HUNG ON FOR DEAR LIFE, WHEN A POLICEMAN WALKED OVER AND SAID, 'COME ON – GET GOING – MOVE ALONG.' AND THE DRUNK SAID, 'NOT YET. I'VE STILL GOT TWENTY MINUTES LEFT!'

COOPER CLASSIC 1

Now, do you know –
I was cleaning out the attic
the other day – with the
wife – filthy, dirty, and
covered with cobwebs –
but she's good to the kids.
And I found…

*(Tommy goes behind table
and reaches down to
bring out…)*

… this old violin and this
oil painting. So I took
them to an expert and
he said to me, 'What
you've got there – you've
got a Stradivarius and a
Rembrandt. Unfortunately…

*(Tommy's eyes survey the audience with a mixture of
disappointment and suspicion, as only his could)*

…Stradivarius was a terrible painter and Rembrandt
made rotten violins!'

*(At which point Tommy pushes the violin through the
canvas and slings them both aside)*

TOMMY'S LUCKY DIP

DO YOU KNOW I HAD A FUNNY DREAM LAST NIGHT?
I DREAMT I WAS A CANNON AND I SHOT OUT OF BED AND
WHEN I GOT UP I REALISED I WAS WALKING FUNNY AND I
SAID TO MYSELF, 'THAT'S FUNNY.' I DID. I SAID, 'THAT'S
FUNNY.' AND I WENT TO THE DOCTOR ABOUT IT AND I
SAID, 'I'M WALKING FUNNY.' HE SAID, 'IF YOU DON'T MIND
ME SAYING SO, YOU'VE GOT ONE LEG SHORTER THAN THE
OTHER.' I SAID, 'I DO MIND YOU SAYING SO.' OH, I DID!
I WAS FIRM. I WAS FIRM. I SAID, 'I DO MIND YOU SAYING
SO.' I SAID, 'I THINK YOU'VE GOT A DOWNRIGHT CHEEK.'
HE SAID, 'NO, YOU'VE GOT A DOWN RIGHT CHEEK.
THAT'S WHY YOU'RE WALKING FUNNY!'

THERE WAS MOTHER BEAR, FATHER BEAR AND BABY BEAR
AND THE BABY BEAR SAID, 'WHO'S BEEN EATING MY
PORRIDGE?' AND THE FATHER BEAR SAID, 'WHO'S BEEN
EATING MY PORRIDGE?' AND THE MOTHER BEAR SAID,
'WHAT'S ALL THE TROUBLE? I HAVEN'T MADE IT YET.'

HERE'S A QUICK JOKE - I MUST TELL YOU THIS - I WANT
TO HEAR IT MYSELF! IT'S ABOUT THE FAITH HEALER AND
HE SAID TO THIS MAN, 'HOW'S YOUR BROTHER?' AND HE
SAID, 'HE'S ILL.' AND THE FAITH HEALER SAID, 'NO, NO,
NO. HE ONLY THINKS HE'S ILL.' HE SAID, 'NO, HE'S ILL -
HE LOOKS ILL - HE LOOKS ILL.' HE SAID, 'NO.' HE SAID,
'I'M TELLING YOU. HE LOOKS ILL - I LOOKED AT HIM THE
OTHER DAY - HE LOOKS ILL.' SO THREE WEEKS LATER HE
MET HIM AGAIN. HE SAID, 'HOW'S YOUR BROTHER?' HE
SAID, 'HE THINKS HE'S DEAD.'

MUSICAL COOPER

I have an electric guitar that doesn't need electricity. It burns coal!!

The other day I bought a piano stool and I've taken it back six times. I turn it in every direction and I still can't get a single note out of it.

I broke my arm and I went to the doctor. And I said, 'Doctor when it's mended will I be able to play the piano?' and he said, 'Of course you will,' and I said, 'That's funny. I couldn't play before.'

> This conductor was giving his orchestra a stiff rehearsal when he dropped his baton. He said 'Trombone player was playing his instrument too loud.' 'Trombone player hasn't got here yet' 'Alright - when he gets here tell him he was playing too loud.'

This conductor was giving his orchestra a stiff rehearsal when he dropped his baton. He said, 'The trombone player was playing his instrument too loud.' Someone said, 'The trombone player hasn't got here yet.'
He said, 'Alright, when he gets here tell him he was playing too loud.'

I'm very musical. A lot of people don't know this, but I was born with a banjo on my knee – the doctors had to operate before I could get my trousers on.

This man said, 'What does your father do?' I said, 'He was a conductor.' He said, 'Musical or on the buses?' I said, 'Neither. He was struck by lightning!'

PHILOSOPHICAL COOPER

Did you know, I read the other day that twenty per cent of driving accidents are caused by drunken drivers? That must mean then that the other eighty per cent are caused by drivers who are stone cold sober. In other words, if all drivers got drunk, there would be far less accidents.

If you drink and drive, remember alcohol and petrol don't mix – well, they do, but the taste's terrible!

If you drive & drink – remember alcohol & petrol dont mix – well it does but taste's terrible!!!

Remember when you drive, don't drink – you may spill it!

It's like garages, isn't it? Wherever they put a petrol pump they find petrol!

Maybe I should copyright myself – people impersonating me all the time. I mean it's not the principle – it's the money!

My father was a great philosopher and he said to me, 'It doesn't matter if you let love slip through your fingers or even money slip through your fingers, but if you let your fingers slip through your fingers you're in trouble.' That's semi-jolly, isn't it?

Let a smile be your umbrella and you'll get soaking wet.

The only good thing about rain is that you don't have to shovel it!

Why do the people you hate most have the best luck?

How do the birds know when you've just cleaned your car?

The waiter is a man who believes that money grows on trays.

Somebody once said that horsepower was a very good thing when only horses had it.

Does a cat wash his face – or does he wash his feet and wipe them on his face?

If you're feeling low, eat a box of Lux – you're bound to bubble over!

Do you know what's embarrassing? When you look through a keyhole and see another eye!

Show me a man with two feet on the ground and I'll show you a man who can't take off his trousers.

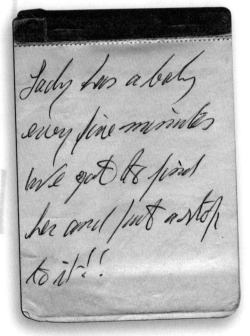

A lady has a baby every five minutes. We've got to find her and put a stop to it.

M is for the million things she gave me...
O means that she's only growing old...
T is for the tears she shed to save me...
H is for her heart so pure of gold...
Put them altogether...
They spell **MOTH**!

The ballet is something I can't understand. All those girls dancing around on their toes. I figure if they want taller girls – why don't they get 'em?

There were six chorus girls. Five married millionaires and one of them married a poor man. And do you know something? She's the only one who's miserable!!

I always say a friend in need is a pest – get rid of him. And if at first you don't succeed, forget it!

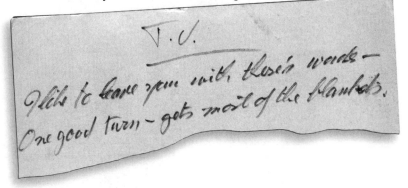

I'd like to leave you with these words – one good turn gets most of the blankets.

MEET THE FAMILY

My boy came towards me the other day with his arms out and he walked slowly towards me. He went 'Dad, dad, dad.' Oh – it was wonderful – he's only fifteen. He'll be sixteen soon, if I let him. Oh dear!

My boy complains about headaches. I told him a thousand times. — when you get out of bed its feet first!!

My boy complains about headaches. I told him a thousand times – when you get out of bed it's feet first!

The other day he had an accident. He went into a barber shop for a haircut and came out with the wrong head!

My daughter is always washing her face. I know that cleanliness is next to godliness, but after she gets through washing her face she irons it!

This mother had eleven children. Her kids got so noisy, so she told them, 'The first one in this house who screams is going to get a mouth full of soap.' And do you know, I can still taste the stuff!

There were eleven of us in our family and we were so poor we used to wear each others' clothes. I didn't mind, but I had ten sisters.

I had a grandfather who passed away when he was 137 years old – *just like that!* No one expected it. His father was really broken up about it!

Do you like my watch? My grandfather sold it to me on his death bed – I gave him a cheque!

I've been looking up my family tree. They were all enjoying their bananas!

My little boy said to me today, he said, 'What do you call a gorilla that's got a banana in each ear?' And I said, 'What do you call a gorilla that's got a banana in each ear?' He said, 'Anything you like – he can't hear you!'

TOMMY AT THE DENTIST

Oh, my teeth itch!

A dentist had to pull a horse's tooth, which he found easy, but the tough part was getting the horse to sit in the chair!

I always wanted to be a dentist, but my hands were too big. Before I could get to the back teeth, I had to pull out all the front teeth.

I went to the dentist. He said my teeth are all right, but my gums have got to come out. He looked at me and I said, 'I've got a terrible pain just up there – see. *(Shows by putting finger in his mouth)* Up there it was. And he said, 'I tell you what I'll do' and I said, 'What's that?' Cos he spoke to me and I said, 'I've got a pain up there.' He said, 'I tell you what I'll do – I'll X-ray it.' So he got these tiny X-rays like that – little small ones like that and he put it up there like that. He put it up there like that. And I'm sitting there like that and he brings this X-ray machine in – see there – and it went *(Makes drilling sound)* like that and he took it out and he looked at it and he said, 'No wonder it hurts – you've got a finger poked up there!'

Cooper à la Carte

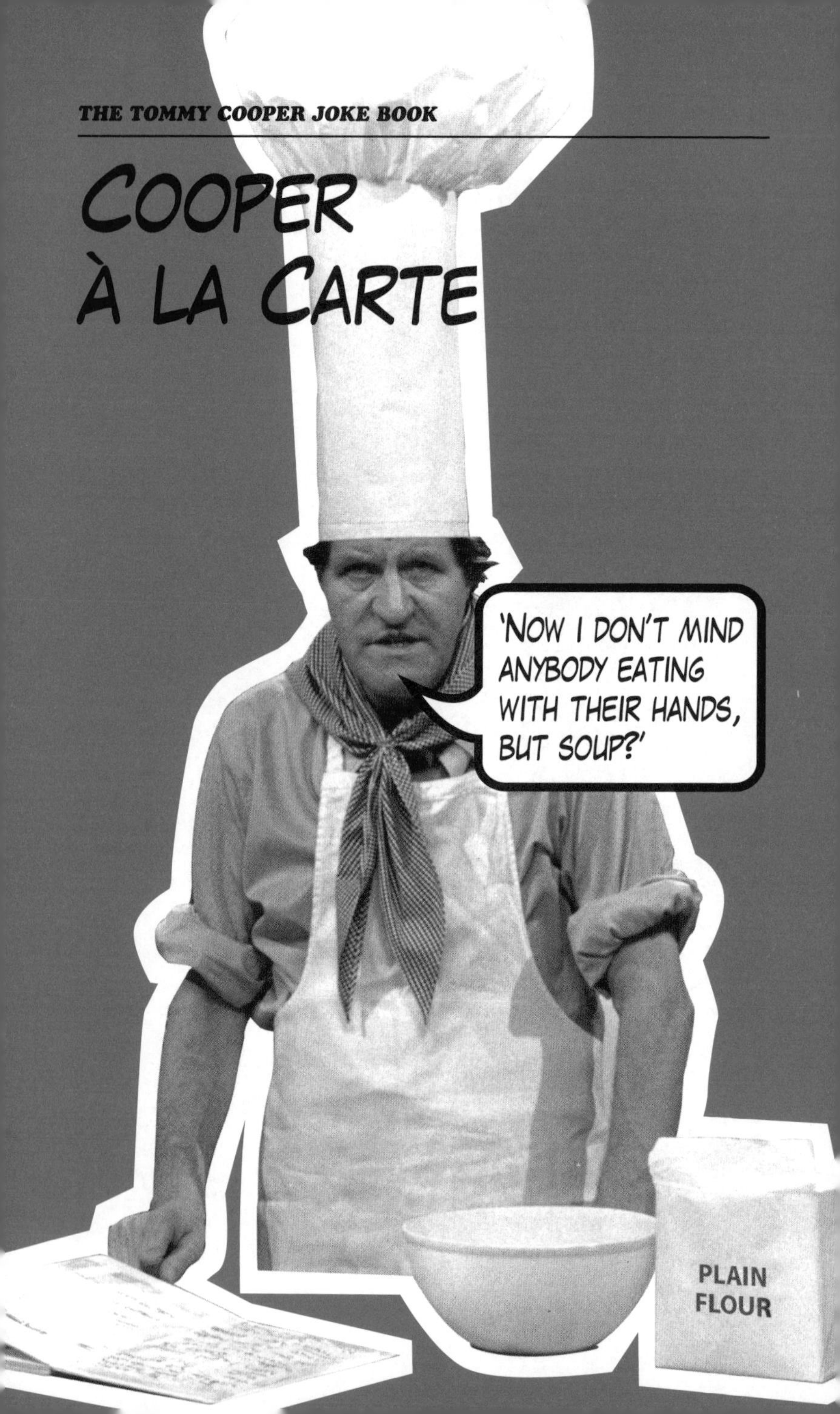

YOU KNOW, I HAD A MEAL LAST NIGHT. I ORDERED EVERYTHING IN FRENCH. I SURPRISED EVERYBODY. IT WAS A CHINESE RESTAURANT.

AND I SAID TO THIS WAITER, I SAID, 'THIS CHICKEN I'VE GOT HERE'S COLD.' HE SAID, 'IT SHOULD BE. IT'S BEEN DEAD TWO WEEKS.' I SAID, 'NOT ONLY THAT,' I SAID, 'IT'S GOT ONE LEG SHORTER THAN THE OTHER.' HE SAID, 'WHAT D'YOU WANT TO DO? EAT IT OR DANCE WITH IT!'

I SAID, 'FORGET THE CHICKEN.' I SAID, 'GIVE ME A LOBSTER.' SO HE BROUGHT THE LOBSTER. I LOOKED AT IT. I SAID, 'JUST A MINUTE,' I SAID, 'IT'S ONLY GOT ONE CLAW.' HE SAID, 'IT'S BEEN IN A FIGHT.' I SAID, 'WELL, GET ME THE WINNER!'

I SAID, 'HAVE YOU GOT FROG'S LEGS?' HE SAID, 'YES.' I SAID, 'WELL, HOP OVER THE COUNTER AND GET ME A CHEESE SANDWICH!'

AND I SAID TO THIS CHINESE WAITER, I SAID, 'TELL ME SOMETHING.' I SAID, 'ARE THERE ANY CHINESE JEWS?' HE SAID, 'I DUNNO. I'LL GO AND FIND OUT.' SO HE WENT AND HE CAME BACK. HE SAID, 'NO. THERE'S ONLY APPLE JUICE, PINEAPPLE JUICE, AND ORANGE JUICE.' THANK YOU!

I SAID, 'WAITER, WHAT'S THAT IN MY SOUP?' HE SAID, 'I'D BETTER CALL THE BOSS, BECAUSE I CAN'T TELL ONE INSECT FROM ANOTHER.'

A GIRL BEHIND THE BAR SAID, 'WHAT WOULD YOU LIKE TO DRINK?' I SAID, 'I'LL HAVE A GIN... AND BITTER LEMON.' SHE SAID, 'HERE'S YOUR GIN AND WHAT DID YOU BITE MY LEMON FOR?'

You know it's not my day! I backed a horse today 20 to 1 – it came in 20 past 4. He was so late coming in he had to tiptoe back to the stables. And the jockey kept hitting him like that with a whip – like that – not like that – like that and the horse said, 'What are you doing that for? There's nobody behind us!'

I bought a greyhound about a month ago. A friend of mine said, 'What are you gonna do with it?' I said, 'I'm gonna race it.' He said, 'By the look of it, I think you'll beat it.'

You know my memory's terrible. I cut myself shaving today and I forgot to bleed.

My back's terrible. I was playing piggyback with my little boy. I fell off!

I get dizzy when I lick an airmail stamp!

I'm superstitious – I won't work a week with a Friday in it!

It's not my night. I've always been unlucky. I had a rocking horse once and it died.

I've got a cigarette lighter that won't go out.

I don't feel so good tonight. In fact, just before the show I met my life insurance agent and he took his calendar back.

I feel terrible tonight. Last night – one bottle of beer and I was out like a light. Someone hit me over the head with it!

I fell off the ironing board – I was pressing my trousers – and I forgot to take them off!"

I fell off the ironing board – I was pressing my trousers and I forgot to take them off!!

My wife and I used to go to race meetings and I was told to cut off a lock of her hair, for luck, for every race. Eventually we had a hundred thousand pounds in the bank and not a hair on her head.

I was there at Woolwich last week – the ferry was about ten feet from the quay. It could have been eleven feet. I think it was eleven feet. So I took a flying leap, cos I've got long legs, and I landed right on it and said to the man, 'I've just made it.' He said, 'You had plenty of time. I was coming in.'

I woke up and I felt awful, I really did. I thought I'd passed away and nobody had told me. And I started to read the paper – like you do – and I looked down the obituary column. I did. I read the whole list and when I saw my name wasn't there, I got up.

STATING THE OBVIOUS

'I FEEL A LITTLE LIGHT-HEADED!'

Tommy walks on stage carrying a portable oil stove...
Thank you very much. They just told me. They said, 'Go out there and warm them up.' Huh huh huh!

This fellow said to me yesterday, 'Do you always drink your gin neat?' I said, 'No. As a matter of fact, sometimes I don't wear a tie and have my shirt hanging out.'

Do you know I've had a pain here all day?
(He reaches inside his jacket and brings out a small square of glass)
Look at that – oh dear!
(He tosses it aside and picks up a golf club)
I joined a golf club last week.
(He separates club into two pieces)
It keeps coming apart!

(He places a piece of tissue paper in a metal dish and applies match ...whoosh!)
Just a flash in the pan!

Oh, my feet are killing me – you know every night when I'm lying in bed they get me right round the throat like that!

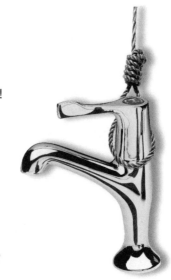

And now a tap dance!
(He picks up string with tap tied on the end and jiggles it about – then picks up glove...)
See that glove...
(He releases another glove, sewn to first glove at the fingertips)

Look, second hand!

(He picks up a skipping rope, looks at it...)
Here we have a skipping rope – so we'll skip that!
(...and throws it away...)

Now, before we go any further, I'd just like to say this. It's a funny word, this. I mean, how many times could you go on stage and this will get a laugh? This, it's a funny word that. Now that, that's funnier than this...

Look, see that *(Tommy holds up left hand and wriggles its fingers)*

– well this one's just the same! *(Repeats with other hand)*

(He puts on a pair of joke spectacles with horns attached)
Look! Horn-rimmed glasses! I should be locked up!

Do you know what the bald-headed man said when he received a comb for Christmas? 'I'll never part with it!'

(A stagehand now walks across carrying one half of a life-size, head-to-toe cardboard cut-out of Tommy…)
That's my half-brother!

I'd like now to show you a photograph of that wonderful escapologist, Houdini. *(He picks up an envelope, takes out a piece of blank card, shows it...*

...and slings it to one side)
He's got away again!

One of the studio staff said, 'Tommy, do you like bathing beauties?' I said, 'I don't know. I've never bathed any!'

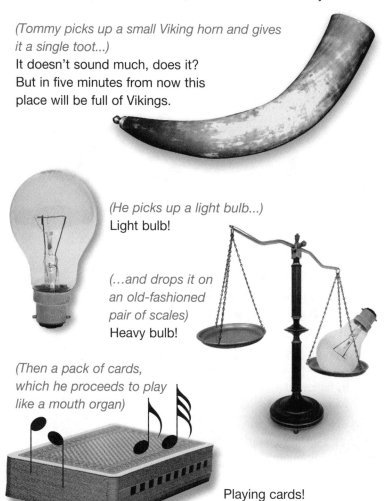

(Tommy picks up a small Viking horn and gives it a single toot...)
It doesn't sound much, does it?
But in five minutes from now this place will be full of Vikings.

(He picks up a light bulb...)
Light bulb!

(...and drops it on an old-fashioned pair of scales)
Heavy bulb!

(Then a pack of cards, which he proceeds to play like a mouth organ)

Playing cards!

When some women feel the urge to love, they get married.
I know a girl who wanted someone to love, so she bought a
German shepherd. Not a dog, a real German shepherd!

(He picks up a stick of pink peppermint seaside rock...)
I will now turn this stick of rock into furniture.
(He breaks it into three pieces...)
One – two – three!

*(...and tosses the three
pieces over his shoulder)*
Three-piece suite! Eh?

Two cannibals were eating
a clown – one said to
the other, 'Does he taste
funny to you?'

Now to finish I'd just
like to sing you one little
song – when you walk
through the storm, with
your head held high – I
did and I fell in a river!

TOMMY THE BOXER

This routine from Tommy's early career reflects his love of the sport. He always said that the best thing about his time serving in the Guards was the boxing, at which he excelled. His height and bulk made him a natural.

I used to be a boxer, but I had to give it up. I couldn't learn to pick up my teeth with gloves on!

I come from a long line of boxers – except my father – he was a Dalmatian!

I'm still in good shape. I can still go ten rounds – as long as someone is buying them!

I used to be a boxer. They used to call me Canvasback Cooper. I did pretty good at the beginning. I won my first ten fights, then I ran into trouble. They made me fight a man! I used to go into the ring vertical and come out horizontal. My best punch was a rabbit punch, but they wouldn't let me fight rabbits.

> Boxing 2
>
> What a fight! When the bell rang, I came out of my corner and threw six straight punches in a row. Then the other fellow came out of his corner. First he threw a right cross, then he threw a left cross. Then came the Red Cross. He came up to about my chin. The trouble was he came up too often.

What a fight! When the bell rang, I came out of my corner and threw six straight punches in a row. Then the other fellow came out of his corner. First he threw a right cross, then he threw a left cross. Then came the Red Cross. He came up to about my chin. The trouble was he came up too often.

In the fifth round I had my opponent worried. He thought he killed me. But in the sixth round I had him covered with blood – mine! I had so much resin on my back that whenever I passed the Albert Hall, the fiddlers used to stand at attention. Then I brought one up from the floor – which is where I happened to be at the time.

> Boxing 3
>
> In the fifth round I had my opponent worried. He thought he killed me. But in the sixth round I had him covered with blood – mine!! I had so much resin on my back that whenever I passed Albert Hall, the fiddles used to stand at attention. Then I brought one up from the floor – which is where I happened to be at the time.

After that fight they gave me a cup – to keep my teeth in. Just before the fight started, my manager yelled in my ear that my opponent beat his wife, kicked his children and starved his mother. That made me really fighting mad. If there's one thing I can't stand, it's someone yelling in my ear!

I wasn't taking any chances. In my right glove I had a horseshoe, a bag of cement and an anvil. Only one thing kept me from winning that fight. I couldn't get my glove off the floor! First I gave him my left. Then I gave him my right. After that I was through. I didn't have anything left for myself!

COOPER CLASSIC 2

There was an Irishman, a Mexican and a German taken prisoner. I don't know where – they were just taken prisoner. And they were ordered to be flogged, see. So they said to the Mexican, 'You can have anything on your back, whatever you like to ease the pain.' So he said, 'I'll have olive oil.' So they rubbed it all over his back like that *(Tommy mimes the application of oil to the prisoner's back)* and they went, 'Crunch – crunch, crunch, crunch.' *(He mimes ferociously with imaginary whip)* 'And crunch!' I put that extra 'Crunch' in! And he flopped on the floor and they dragged him out. And it was the German's turn and he stood there like that. *(Tommy stands rigid to attention)* And they said, 'What do you want on your back?' He said, 'Nein.' That means 'Nothing,' doesn't it? So they got the whip and they went, 'Crunch, crunch – crunch, crunch, like that.' *(Tommy mimes, even more agitated than before)* He just stood there. He didn't bat an eyelid, didn't bat an eyelid. And it was the Irishman's turn and they said, 'What do you want on your back?' He said, 'I'll have the German!'

BACK WITH THE AUDIENCE

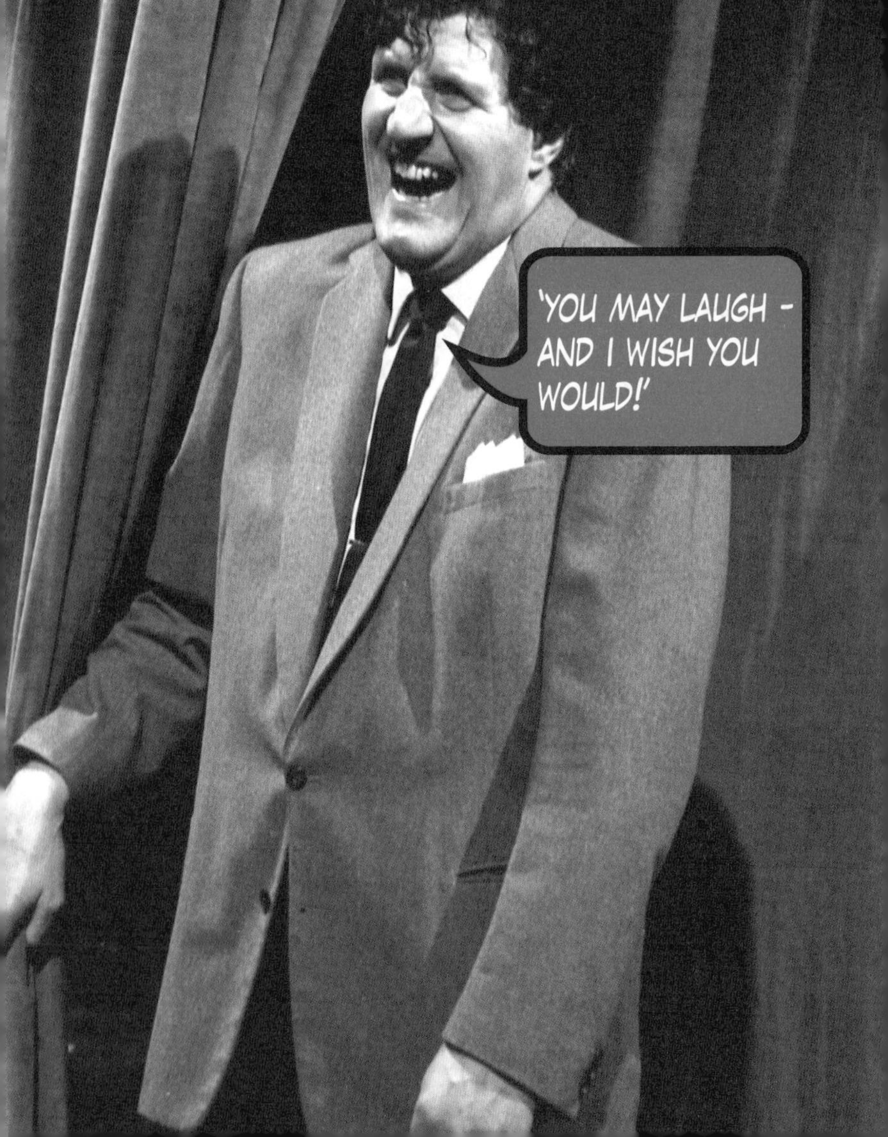

It's only natural to be nervous at the beginning of a show – but please don't be. I want you to enjoy yourselves this evening. There is no need to laugh or applaud. Just forget that I'm the sole support of a wife and a family. Forget that I'm pure at heart. Forget that I served the country for five desperate years in a lonely foxhole in the steaming jungles of Burma. Forget all that! If you don't want to laugh or applaud, I won't care!

Wouldn't it be funny if I looked up and you were all gone? I've had a request, but I'm not leaving until I'm good and ready.

They gave me a lovely dressing room – a nail. That's the first time I ever had a dressing room where I have to tip the attendant.

I wish I had a Polaroid camera so that I could get a close-up of that joke dying.

We've got a brilliant show for you tonight. Brilliant. The best ever. And if I'm telling you one word of a lie, may I be struck down on this very spot. *(Tommy moves away from the spot and looks upward…)*

What a wonderful audience – this will stay in my memory right up until seven a.m. tomorrow morning.

Thanks for coming in for my audition. Next week I'm going back in show business.

Now get ready for this one – it's one of the first jokes I ever stole.

When I'm not doing tricks, I put on a floor show –
I demonstrate vacuum cleaners!

A little boy said to me, 'One reason I like watching your show is because as soon as it's over a better one comes on!'

Come back tomorrow night. I'll be opening in person.

At least you can try and laugh from memory.

I see we have a very reserved group here, so if I happen to say something funny just nod and I'll understand.

One more joke like that and my picture won't be in the lobby anymore – I'll be hanging out there in person.

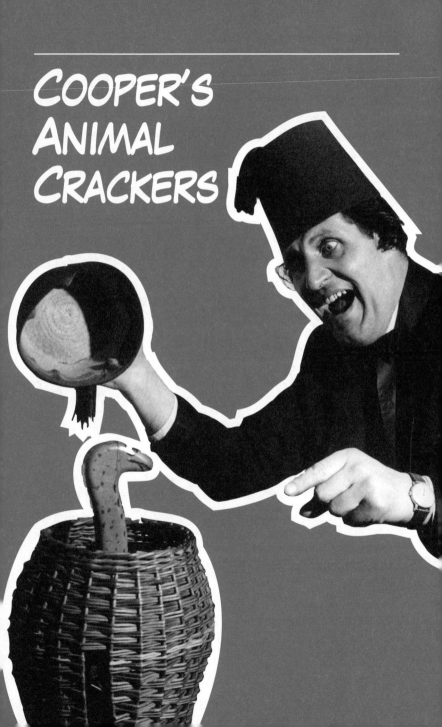

COOPER'S
ANIMAL
CRACKERS

Do you know, I was walking down the street the other day.
I know a lot of people say that, but I was. And I saw this little
fence so I looked over it and there was this little chicken, a
little Rhode Island Red, and he must have been psychic
because he looked up and went, 'Cluck, cluck.' So I went,
'Cluck, cluck' and then he went, 'Cluck, cluck.' So I went,
'Cluck, cluck.' And this policeman came along and he arrested
us both for using foul language!

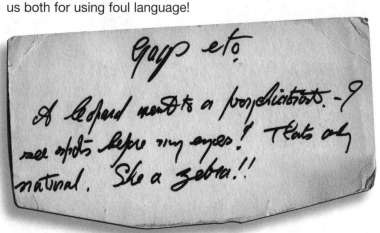

A leopard went to see a psychiatrist. He said, 'Every time I
look at my wife I see spots before my eyes.' The psychiatrist
said, 'That's only natural.' He said, 'But doctor, she's a zebra.'

Do you know that a grizzly bear crawls into a cave and sleeps
for six months? Do you know why? Who's going to wake him
up?

This elephant trod on a mouse. The giraffe said, 'Why did you
do that?' He said, 'I didn't mean to. I only meant to trip him up.'

Elephants are remarkable
animals? They travel for miles,
& miles over mountains and
through the jungles to a place
where they're going to die &
They die there — The Trip Kills
'em.!!

Elephants are remarkable animals. They travel for miles and miles over mountains and through the jungles to a place where they're going to die and they die there – the trip kills 'em!

There's a man having a barbecue in the front garden. So he's turning the spit like this and the flames are getting higher and higher – higher and higher, see – and he's singing. 'Oh sole mio… O sole mio, farewell.' And the flames are getting higher and higher and this drunk walks by and says, 'Your singing's alright, but your monkey's on fire!'

Farmer Brown had a parrot and he took him to town and he bought a crate of chickens. So he's coming back and he turns around and the parrot is sitting on the back – and all the chickens are walking. The parrot said, 'Look girls, when you listen to reason, you can ride!'

TOMMY AND THE LAW

I WAS ON MY WAY HOME FROM THE THEATRE THE OTHER NIGHT. I WAS WALKING HOME WITH THESE TWO SUITCASES, SEE, AND THIS POLICEMAN CAME UP TO ME AND IT'S AFTER MIDNIGHT AND THE POLICEMEN STOP YOU TO SEE WHAT YOU'VE GOT INSIDE. SO THIS POLICEMAN STOPPED ME, YOU SEE, AND HE SAID, 'WHAT HAVE YOU GOT IN THAT CASE THERE?' A BIT HARSH HE WAS. I SAID, 'WHAT HAVE I GOT IN THERE?' HE SAID, 'YES.' I SAID, 'IN THERE, I'VE GOT SUGAR FOR MY TEA!' HE SAID, 'AND WHAT HAVE YOU GOT IN THE OTHER ONE?' I SAID, 'IN THAT ONE I'VE GOT SUGAR FOR MY COFFEE.' AND THEN HE TOOK OUT HIS TRUNCHEON AND WENT 'BOOM'... (TOMMY MIMES STRIKING AND BEING DAZED AS A RESULT)...'THERE'S A LUMP FOR YOUR COCOA!'

I WAS WALKING HOME THE OTHER NIGHT. A MAN CAME OUT OF A DOORWAY. HE SAID, 'HAVE YOU SEEN A POLICEMAN AROUND HERE?' I SAID, 'NO.' HE SAID, 'STICK 'EM UP.'

DID YOU HEAR THE JOKE ABOUT THE POLICEMAN WHO STOPPED THIS MAN? HE SAID, 'RIGHT, GET OUT OF THE CAR. GET OUT.' HE SAID, 'I WANT YOU TO BLOW INTO THIS.' SO THE FELLOW WENT (TOMMY BLOWS) AND AS HE DID A BIG HORN CAME OUT OF HIS HEAD. SO HE SAID, 'DO IT AGAIN.' SO HE WENT (TOMMY BLOWS AGAIN) AND ANOTHER HORN CAME OUT. HE SAID, 'WHAT HAVE YOU BEEN DRINKING?' HE SAID, 'BOVRIL!'

DID YOU HEAR THE ONE ABOUT THE NEAR-SIGHTED BANK ROBBER. HE WENT INTO THE BANK. HE SAID, 'STICK EM UP.' *(TOMMY MIMES ACCORDINGLY)* 'ARE THEY UP?' HUH HUH HUH.

Man fell out of a tenth-story window. He's lying on the ground with a big crowd around him a policeman walks over and says – What happened? The man says, I don't know, I just got here!

A MAN FELL OUT OF A TEN-STOREY WINDOW. HE'S LYING ON THE GROUND WITH A BIG CROWD AROUND HIM. A POLICEMAN WALKS OVER AND SAYS, 'WHAT HAPPENED?' THE MAN SAYS, 'I DON'T KNOW. I JUST GOT HERE!'

THERE'S THIS FELLOW AND HE'S ROWING UP THE ROAD LIKE THAT. *(TOMMY MIMES ROWING ACTION)* NOT LIKE THAT, LIKE THAT! SO HE'S ROWING UP THE ROAD LIKE THAT, AND THIS POLICEMAN COMES UP TO HIM AND SAYS, 'WHAT ARE YOU DOING?' AND HE SAYS, 'I'M ROWING UP THE ROAD.' AND THE POLICEMAN SAYS, 'YOU HAVEN'T GOT A BOAT.' AND HE SAYS, 'OH, HAVE I NOT!' *(TOMMY MIMES AS IF SWIMMING FOR HIS LIFE!)*

MORE LAUGHTER ALLSORTS

Two guys were out in the passage talking. One said to the other, 'I hear we might be going out on strike – what are we striking for this time?' He said, 'Shorter hours.' The other replied, 'I'm in favour of that – I always thought sixty minutes was too long!'

There's a man in a country lane, and he's in snow up to here *(Tommy holds his hand at chest height)* – up to here like that see, and a man walks up to him and says, 'Dear, oh dear! Don't worry – I'll get a shovel and I'll get you out.' The man says, 'Get a big one – I'm sitting on a horse!'

A man walks down the street with a big red beard and two big horns coming out of his head. He knocks on a door and a woman answers. He says, 'I'm the Danish Bacon Viking. Do you eat Danish Bacon?' She said, 'No fear – if that's what it does for you!'

The taxi driver said, 'I'll take the kids for nothing.' The father turned to the kids and said, 'Okay – jump in, children, and have a nice ride. Your Mother and I will take the tube and see you there!'

There was this fellow. One day his wife said, 'Get out of bed and get a job.' His friend said, 'So what happened? Did you go out and get a job?' and he said, 'Are you kidding? Where can you find a job at five o'clock in the afternoon?'

TOMMY
GOES
ABROAD

Do you know I went to see my travel agent the other day, about my holidays, and I saw a picture of Majorca on the wall, and I said, 'I want to go there.' So he pinned me to the wall! But seriously, I went to Majorca and we went by plane – it's the only way to fly. And you know I always sit in the back, because you never hear of a plane backing into a mountain! It was the biggest thrill of my life when I stepped off that plane – it was still in the air! And I was looking out the window like that – it may have been like that! – no, it was like that – and I saw a man coming down in a parachute and he went like that to me. *(Tommy beckons with his fingers)* I said, 'I'm alright.' He said, 'Please yourself – I'm the pilot.' And it got a little bit rough in the air pockets like that and the plane was all over the place like that. *(He mimes with his arms outstretched)* And there was a little old lady sitting there in the plane and she got so nervous she started to pray and she looked at me and she said, 'Do something religious.' So I did. I took up a collection. And we're coming down to land fast – like that – fast – and it affects your ears, doesn't it? They go all funny, don't they? And the girl came in and gave me chewing gum. That's what they gave me – chewing gum – for the ears. Took me two days to get it out! And while I was there – in Majorca – I went into this bar, and all along the top of the bar were these bulls' heads, and right there in the middle there was this big bull's head. I mean the others were big, but this was really big. You know what I mean. And I said to the barman, 'That's a big bull.' And he said, 'I know, there's a sad story behind that bull.' And he looked like that *(Tommy does sad gesture)* and I said, 'Really?' and he said, 'That bull killed my brother.' I said, 'Really – was he a bull fighter?' He said, 'No. He walked in here one day and it fell on his head.'

RISQUÉ COOPER

My uncle was 83 and wanted to marry a girl of nineteen. The doctor said, 'This could be fatal.' He said, 'If she dies, she dies!'

An agent said to a producer, 'I've got a girl who wears a size 102 bra!' The producer said, 'A 102 size brassiere? What does she do?' and the agent said, 'She tries to stand up.'

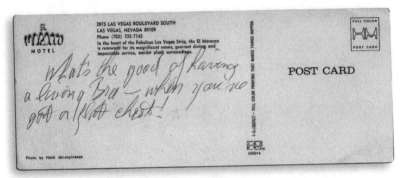

What's the good of a having a living bra when you've got a flat chest?

This man said to the policeman, 'This man started to hug me, kiss me, and embrace me!' The policeman said, 'Why didn't you run away?' He said, 'How could I in my high heels?'

Show me a milkman with high heels and I'll show you a Dairy Queen!

Do you know the difference between bongo drums and sex? Well, you can't beat sex.

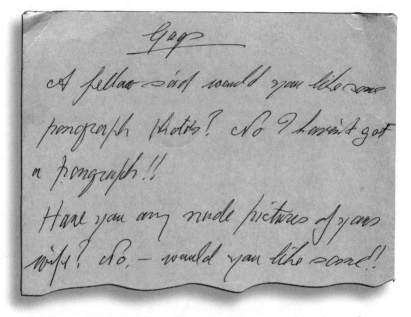

A fellow said, 'Would you like some pornographic photos?
I said, 'No, I haven't got a pornograph!!'

He said, 'Have you any nude pictures of your wife?' I said,
'No.' He said, 'Would you like some?'

I'm reading a book called 'Sex before 20.' Personally I don't
like audiences.

If sex is a pain in the neck, you're doing it wrong.

If you think this is dull, you ought to see my love life.

My timing is off lately. When I sit down to eat I get sexy!
When I go to bed I get hungry!

COOPER CLASSIC 3

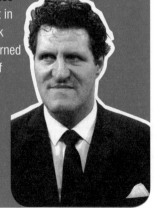

Now there's something I wanna say.
There's a man went into a pub see and got a pint of beer. He drank the beer, put the glass on the counter, turned to the people on the right and said, 'You're a bunch of idiots' and he turned to the people on the left and he said, 'You're a bunch of fools' and he walked out. Next night he's back. Gets a pint, puts the glass on the counter and he turns to the right and he says, 'You're a bunch of idiots' and to the left, 'You're a bunch of fools' and he walks out. There was a man sitting there. And he said, 'Look, if he comes in tomorrow night – he may not come in – I don't know.' Well you don't know, do you? Well he may or he may not. Well you can't blame me, can you? I don't care. I don't know the fellow. I don't care if he comes in. Makes no difference to me. (Tommy's voice gets more strangulated as he pleads) But in he came. He came in, got the beer, drank the beer, put the glass on the counter, turned to the people. He said, 'You're a bunch of idiots and you're a bunch of fools.' And this man said, 'Just a minute. I'm not a fool.' He said, 'Well, join the idiots over there then.' Thank you.

MORE ONE-LINERS

I FEEL GOOD TONIGHT – I COULD CRUSH A GRAPE!

YOU KNOW, I JUST RECEIVED A LETTER FROM BILL BAILEY AND HE'S NOT COMING HOME!

I'M ON A WHISKEY DIET – LAST WEEK I LOST THREE DAYS.

I WENT TO AN OLD FILM YESTERDAY. BEN HUR. I LIKED BEN, COULDN'T STAND HER.

OH, I'VE GOT SOMETHING IN MY EYE. IT'S MY FINGER!

I FEEL SO NERVOUS TONIGHT, I MIGHT GET A TRICK RIGHT.

(ADDRESSED TO RUBBER CHICKEN) STOP HANGING ABOUT AND GET DRESSED!

I ALWAYS SAY DO UNTO OTHERS, BUT DO IT FAST.

THIS COULD DRIVE ME SANE.

ON THE OTHER HAND – I'VE GOT FOUR FINGERS AND A THUMB.

NOW THIS TRICK STARTS VERY SLOWLY AND GRADUALLY PETERS OUT.

BEFORE I GO I WOULD LIKE TO BE SERIOUS FOR A MOMENT. THAT'S ENOUGH!

MY LITTLE BOY LOVES THIS. I LOVE KIDS – I WENT TO SCHOOL WITH THEM.

COURTING COOPER

I'll never forget the first time we met. She was sitting on top of Waterloo Bridge – dangling her feet in the water. She cocked one eye at me and I cocked one eye at her and there we stood together cockeyed. And she had most unusual lips – both on top – and long blonde wavy hair – all down her back. None on her head – all down her back. And she had a very cute little button nose – I used to like the way it turned up, then down, then sideways – but I loved her and we had some wonderful happy times together. We used to go on the beach. She gave me a wave – I've still got it at home in a bucket. We used to go on the sands and play little games together. She used to bury me in the sand and then I buried her in the sand and one of these days I'm gonna go back and dig her up. And then she said she was hungry – so I bought her a stick of rock – and she bit it. And she went, 'Oh!' It wasn't quite so loud as that – it was more, 'Oh!' And then she started to cry a bit. I said, 'What's the matter, love?' She said, 'I've broken a tooth.' I said, 'Don't worry – you've got one left.' And when she stood up she had bow legs – she used to walk like that. I said to her, 'Why don't you learn to play the cello?' So I said to myself I'll take her to get some lovely teeth. So I got the best set of false teeth that money can buy. They looked beautiful – beautiful – and then after all that *(Tommy starts to cry)* – the money I spent on her – she left me – left me *(He's weeping buckets now)*. And a year later I met her again and she came towards me and she just stood there and laughed at me – laughed at me – with my own teeth!

BACK AT THE
DOCTOR'S

Oh dear – what a day I've had! I went to see my doctor. I had
to – he's ill. He said, 'I want you to lie down on the couch.'
I said, 'What for?' He said, 'I want to sweep up.'

I said, 'But seriously, doctor, I have broken my arm in several
places.' He said, 'Well, you shouldn't go to those places.'

I said, 'It hurts me when I do this.' *(Tommy raises arm)*
He said, 'Well, don't do it!'

And I said, 'Doctor, doctor, it hurts when I do this *(Tommy
presses his elbow with his finger)*, and it hurts when I do this
(He presses his ear with his finger), and it hurts when I do this.'
(He presses his chest with his finger) I said, 'What have I done?'
He said, 'Broken your finger.'

Doctor: you will live to be seventy. P. says I am seventy. D. What did I tell you.

The doctor said to the patient, 'You will live to be seventy.'
The patient said, 'I am seventy.' The doctor said, 'What did
I tell you?'

My doctor goes to about six or seven hospitals a week.
He's a very sick doctor.

Yesterday I went round to the doctor. There was nothing wrong
with me – I just felt like sticking my tongue out at somebody.

What a doctor! For ten minutes he listened with a stethoscope – then he said, 'Just as I thought – dandruff!'

I've used saccharine for years and my doctor told me I had artificial diabetes!

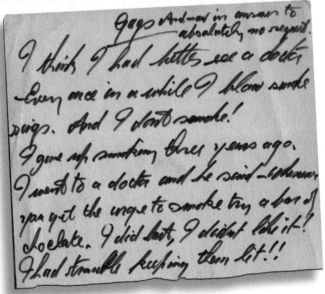

I think I had better see a doctor. Every once in a while I blow smoke rings – and I don't smoke!

I gave up smoking three years ago. I went to my doctor and he said, 'Whenever you get the urge to smoke, try a bar of chocolate.' I did, but I didn't like it. I had trouble keeping them lit!

I read of a doctor whose prescriptions were so illegible that a patient used one for two years as a Railway Pass, got into theatres and football cup ties with it, and finally gave it to his daughter who played it on the piano and won a scholarship to the Royal College of Music!

BACK IN THE JUNGLE

Now, here's a quick joke.

It was in the jungle see – in the jungle – and there was a hyena and he's talking to this monkey and he said, 'You see that little passage, that little narrow way down there – you see that big clump of trees and bushes,' and this monkey said, 'Yes.' And he said, 'Well, I go home that way every night. I don't have to, but you know it's a short cut for me and I go home' and he said, 'Every time I get to that bunch of trees there this lion jumps out and throws me all over the place.' He said, 'I don't know why he picks on me. Every time he keeps throwing me about and bashing me about and then he goes.' And he said, 'It's funny. D'you know what I mean?' So this monkey said, 'I know what you mean.' He said, 'I'll tell you what – I'll come over here tonight – you know – to protect you.' So the hyena said, 'Would you?' The monkey said, 'Yes.' So they shook hands on it – nothing in writing – and they started to walk down towards this clump of trees, see – huh, huh, huh – I can't help laughing. I know what's coming next! – and they got down to this clump of trees and he was just gonna turn like that and this lion turned and jumped out and got this hyena and went 'boom boom boom' and this monkey went right up the tree and left him there looking at him like that. And he was looking at him like that and all of a sudden this lion went 'boom boom' and left this hyena on his back like that – it may have been like that – no, it was like that – and then the monkey came down and was standing beside him and this hyena's like that and he looks up at this monkey and he said, 'What happened? I thought you were gonna help me.' He said, 'Well, I was, but when I looked down, you were laughing so much, I thought you were winning!'

THE TOMMY COOPER JOKE BOOK

THE MOST FAMOUS MAN IN BRITAIN

TVTime

6p

Time

TOMMY COOPER

MY FANS

Join the £10,000 search for

BRITAIN'S BRIGHTEST WEEKLY

4½d EVERY WEDNESDAY

TV mirror

AND

DISC NEWS

NOVEMBER 29, 1958 (276)

GODFREY WINN
meets
BERNARD
"Popeye"
BRESSLAW

THE FIEND IN
TOMMY COOPER

BERYL GREY:
Girl With The
Laughing Legs

TALK ABOUT BEING RECOGNISED. I SHALL NEVER FORGET
- I WAS GOING TO PLAY LEEDS, JUST OUTSIDE LEEDS,
AND I WAS GOING UP BY PLANE. ANYWAY, IT GOT FOGGY
AND WE WERE DIVERTED TO MANCHESTER. I WAS REALLY
CROSS ABOUT IT, SO I GOT ALL MY PROPS AND CASES
TOGETHER AND I THOUGHT I'LL GO AND HAVE A DRINK
IN THE BAR. TRUE. AND I'M STANDING THERE AND NOT
FEELING TOO HAPPY ABOUT IT AND A YOUNG FELLOW
CAME UP TO ME AND SAID, 'HELLO. WHAT ARE YOU
DOING HERE THEN?' NOW, THERE'S A LOT OF PEOPLE
WALKING ABOUT, SEE, AND I SAID, 'WHAT AM I DOING
HERE?' HE SAID, 'YES. WHAT ARE YOU DOING HERE?'
AND I SAID, 'I TELL YOU WHAT,' I SAID, 'I'VE COME
FROM LONDON, AND I LIVE IN CHISWICK, AND I GOT
FED UP WITH WALKING AROUND THERE, SO I THOUGHT
I'D COME UP HERE TO WALK AROUND HERE.' HE SAID,
'OH! HOW LONG YOU GONNA DO THAT FOR THEN?'
AND I SAID, 'TILL I GET FED UP HERE, THEN I'LL GO
BACK TO CHISWICK AND WALK AROUND THERE AGAIN!'
THE PINHEAD!

YOU KNOW, A CHAP CAME OVER TO ME IN THE PUB
THE OTHER DAY AND SAID, 'I SAW YOU IN CORONATION
STREET LAST WEEK... GREAT!' 'SORRY,' I SAID, 'I WASN'T
IN CORONATION STREET.' 'I'M SURE I SAW YOU IN
CORONATION STREET,' HE INSISTED. I STILL SHOOK MY
HEAD. THEN HE THOUGHT HARD FOR A WHILE, GRIPPED
MY ARM AND SAID, 'NO, THAT'S RIGHT - SAW YOU IN
SAINSBURY'S.'

ENCORE FOR MAXIE!

X. In the desert I met a Mummy —
I think she was looking for her
Daddy. She came right up to me and
said Favio, my Favio. I said I'm
not your Favio — She said, who are
you? I said, I'm ... I am
I come here for a ...
and ginte. She ...
my eyes, what ...
I've got big eyes ...
looking all over ...
She looked into ...
for 2 Thousand ...
for this ...
five 2 Thousand ...

She looked into my eyes and said
Wattill dan gotterd. I gotta also
wulhde than.' I said her how
have you got to go — she said
half a degree — and when I got there
I was in the second division — Playing
for Chelsea. — We started to walk
across the desert — five days and
five nights — we came to a tent — I
stood outside the tent — I wouldn't go in.
2 Thousand years, old she was! We
stood outside the tent — She said
Thy people shall be my people
and my people shall be thy
people. Said mine — we said
they could have been anybody's

I always have a wonderful time when I go on my holidays because I haven't got one of those wives who says, 'Where have you been? How much have you spent? Who have you been with?' She doesn't say that. She comes with me!

But she didn't come with me this time. I went to Africa, the north of Africa, and do you know the first thing I saw in the desert? A mummy. I think she was looking for her daddy! She came right up to me and said, 'Pharaoh, my Pharaoh.' I said, 'I'm not your Pharaoh.' She said, 'Who are you?' I said, 'I'm Mrs Cooper's son. I came here for a little bit of peace and quiet.' She kept on looking at my eyes. What was she after? My lashes? I've got big eyes. That's my mother's fault – looking all over England for my father! She looked into my eyes and said, 'For two thousand years I've waited for this moment. I am a blaze of fire.' I said, 'For two thousand years? You must be hungry. I'll get you some dates!' She looked into my eyes and said, 'Whither thou goest, I goest also whither thou.'

I said, 'How far have you got to go?' She said, 'Half a league' and when we got there I was in the second division – playing for Chelsea! We started to walk across the desert – five days and five nights – then we came to a tent. I stood outside the tent. I wouldn't go in. Two thousand years old she was! We stood outside the tent. She said, 'Thy people shall be my people and my people shall be thy people.' And when we looked they could have been anybody's!

COOPER CLASSIC 4

THERE WAS AN ENGLISHMAN, A SCOTSMAN AND AN IRISHMAN AND THEY WERE ARRESTED FOR BEING DRUNK IN THE STREET. SO THEY SAID – ONE OF THEM SAID – I'LL TELL YOU WHAT WE'LL DO – WE'LL GIVE ASSUMED NAMES.' THE OTHERS SAID (SLURRED), 'GOOD IDEA, YES.' SO THE POLICEMAN SAID TO THE ENGLISHMAN, 'WHAT'S YOUR NAME?' SO THE ENGLISHMAN LOOKED AROUND AT THE SHOPS AND SAW MARKS AND SPENCER, SO HE SAID, 'MARK SPENCER.' AND THE POLICEMAN SAID TO THE SCOTSMAN, 'WHAT'S YOUR NAME?' AND HE LOOKED AND HE SAW TIMOTHY WHITES, SO HE SAID, 'TIM WHITE.' AND HE SAID TO THE IRISHMAN, 'WHAT'S YOUR NAME?' AND HE LOOKED AND SAID, 'KENTUCKY FRIED CHICKEN.'

TOMMY GOES SHOPPING

Do you know I went window shopping today. I bought four windows. And I went to the pet shop and said, 'I'd like to buy a wasp please' and he said, 'We don't sell wasps.' So I said, 'Well, you've got one in the window.'

Then I went to buy some pork chops. I told the butcher to make them lean. He said, 'Which way?'

I went across to the barber shop. I said, 'How much is a hair cut?' He said, 'Twenty quid.' I said, 'How much is a shave?' He said, 'A fiver.' I said, 'Shave my head.'

The barber said to me, 'After you finish shaving, what do you want on your face?' I said, 'Leave the nose.' And he was slow. He was so slow. He looked at me. He said, 'Do you know your hair's turning grey?' I said, 'Well get a move on.'

I went into a chemist's and I said, 'Have you got anything for a headache?' He said, 'Yes.' So he gave me something and I paid him and he said, 'I toss you double or nothing.' So I lost. I walked out with two headaches!

These adverts are silly, aren't they? I saw one the other day. It said, 'Take this wonderful powder for a headache.' I mean, who wants a headache? And I went into a chemist's and I said to the man behind the counter – he was right down behind – I couldn't see him – I said, 'Excuse me, have you got anything for hiccoughs?' I said, *(Tommy raises his voice)* 'Excuse me' – I was a bit harsh – 'have you got anything for hiccoughs? (At the top of his voice) Have you got anything for hiccoughs?' And he jumped up and he hit me right across the face with a cloth. And I said, 'What did you do that for?' 'There you are,' he said, 'you haven't got hiccoughs now, have you?' I said, 'I never had them – it's for my wife out in the car.'

MEET THE
WIFE AGAIN

My wife has a bad memory – she remembers everything!

The meals she cooks put colour in your face – purple!

I said to my wife, 'I can't eat this beef stew.' She said, 'Shut up! It's custard pie.'

I met my wife at a dance – I thought she was home with the kids. If she ever finds out she'll kill me.

One morning she ran after the dustman and said, 'Am I too late for the dustcart?' He said, 'No – jump in!!'

She puts on cream an inch thick – curlers in her hair – fishing net over the whole thing. She said, 'Kiss me.' I said, 'Take me to your leader!'

I remember the night I had a wreck in my car – now I'm sorry I married her.

She said, 'I've left the car in the dining room.' I said, 'How did you get the car in the dining room?' She said, 'It was easy. I made a left turn when I came out of the kitchen.'

Talk about driving – Once she left the garage at some miles an hour – Then she came back – She forgot the car!!

Talk about driving. Once she left the garage at fifty miles an hour. Then she came back. She forgot the car!

I took her to this restaurant and she said she wasn't hungry. So she asked for a side dish – a side of beef!

I asked the waiter, 'What can I get for my wife?' He said, 'I don't know. What are you asking for her?'

The doctor said my wife and I needed plenty of exercise – so I bought myself some golf clubs and my wife a lawn mower!

I got my wife a new home perm waving outfit. I hit her over the head with a sheet of corrugated iron!

She bit into an apple and broke two teeth. I said, 'Don't get excited, love. You've still got one left.'

My wife said, 'I saved myself for you.' I said, 'You didn't have to save so much.' She said, 'I was Miss England.' I said, 'And a part of Wales too!!'

TOMMY THE FILM STAR

When I was in Hollywood I made two pictures – face forward and sideways.

While I was there I had a long talk with Elizabeth Taylor – she said, 'No!'

You know I've just been offered a part in a film. I have really.

And it's a very sympathetic part – a very sympathetic part. I'll give you a rough idea of what it is. The scene opens like that. *(Tommy spreads out his arms)* There's a thatched cottage all made of thatch and there are a lot of violins going. *(He hums appropriate sound effects)* It'll be better than that – I'm just making it up! And there's a dear old lady in an armchair there and a dear old man sitting in an armchair there. There's a baby in the cot over there and a dog on the mat. And I have this very sympathetic part. I creep in through the door and hit the old man on the top of the head – see – and he doesn't say much. He just says, 'Ooh!' It isn't loud – just, 'Ooh!' Then I stab the lady in the back. She doesn't like it. Then I strangle the baby. Now this is where the sympathetic part comes in. On the way out I pat the dog!

COOPER
THE POET

IT'S EASY TO GRIN WHEN YOUR SHIP COMES IN
AND LIFE IS A HAPPY LOT,
BUT THE MAN WORTHWHILE IS THE MAN WHO CAN SMILE
WHEN HIS SHIRT CREEPS UP IN A KNOT.

HUMPTY DUMPTY SAT ON A WALL
HUMPTY DUMPTY HAD A GREAT FALL
ALL THE KING'S HORSES
AND ALL THE KING'S MEN SAID,
'OH, TO HELL WITH IT!'

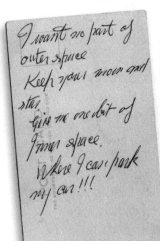

THERE WAS A SCOTSMAN
NAMED ANDY.
HE WENT TO A PUB FOR A SHANDY.
HE BLEW OFF THE FROTH,
USED HIS KILT FOR A CLOTH,
AND THE BARMAN SAID,
'ANDY, THAT'S HANDY.'

I WANT NO PART OF OUTER SPACE
KEEP YOUR MOON AND STAR
GIVE ME ONE BIT OF INNER SPACE
WHERE I CAN PARK MY CAR!

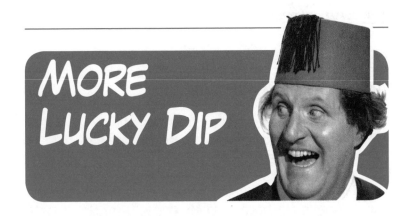

MORE LUCKY DIP

PEOPLE ALWAYS ASK ME WHAT I'M LIKE OFF STAGE. WELL, I'VE GOT QUITE A FEW HOBBIES, YOU KNOW. ONE OF MY HOBBIES - I'M A COLLECTOR. I COLLECT DUST. AND I DO PAINTING TOO. YOU KNOW HOW PEOPLE PAINT BANANAS, ORANGES, AND APPLES? WELL, I PAINT THE JUICE!

DID YOU HEAR ABOUT THE MILLIONAIRE, WHO SAID TO HIS CHAUFFEUR, 'DRIVE OFF THE CLIFFS, JAMES. I'M COMMITTING SUICIDE'?

THIS OLD MAN SAID, 'I HAVEN'T TASTED FOOD FOR WEEKS.' I SAID, 'DON'T WORRY. IT STILL TASTES THE SAME.'

THERE'S A NEW KIND OF RUSSIAN ROULETTE - YOU GET SIX COBRAS IN A ROOM AND YOU PLAY A FLUTE. ONE OF THEM IS DEAF!'

TWO ZULUS WERE TALKING. ONE SAID, 'I DON'T LIKE MY WIFE.' THE OTHER SAID, 'WELL, JUST EAT THE VEGETABLES.'

I USED TO WASH MY HAIR IN VINEGAR. I DID. BUT I GAVE IT UP. THE CHIPS KEPT GETTING IN THE WAY!

I KNOCKED SOMEONE DOWN ON MY BIKE THE OTHER DAY. HE SAID, 'CAN'T YOU RING THE BELL?' I SAID, I CAN RING THE BELL – BUT I CAN'T RIDE THE BIKE!'

THIS WOMAN WENT TO THE DOCTOR. HE SAID, 'YOU'VE GOT A BAD BACK.' SHE SAID, 'I WANT A SECOND OPINION.' HE SAID, 'WELL, YOU'RE UGLY AS WELL.'

I WAS IN THIS HOTEL. I RANG DOWN TO THE MANAGER AND SAID, 'THERE'S NO CEILING TO MY ROOM.' HE SAID, 'THAT'S ALRIGHT. THE MAN ABOVE YOU DOESN'T WALK ABOUT MUCH.'

THIS GUY CAN'T STAND HEIGHTS. HE'S THE ONLY FELLOW I KNOW WHO TAKES ALONG A TANK OF OXYGEN TO PAINT THE LIVING ROOM CEILING.

I THINK THE MAID IS DISHONEST. I JUST FOUND OUT TWO OF THE TOWELS I SWIPED FROM A MANCHESTER HOTEL ARE MISSING.

SOMEBODY RANG MY WIFE AND SAID, 'I SAW YOUR HUSBAND ON THE BEACH WITH A BLONDE ON HIS ARM.' SHE SAID, 'WHAT DO YOU EXPECT AT HIS AGE – A BUCKET AND SPADE?'

LAST WEEK AN INSURANCE MANAGER CAME UP TO ME AND I SAID, 'I'M SORRY. I'VE GOT PLENTY OF INSURANCE.' HE SAID, 'NO, JUST LISTEN TO ME FIRST.' HE SAID, 'ARE YOU LISTENING?' I SAID, 'I AM.' I WAS! AND I LOOKED AT HIM LIKE THAT – SQUARE IN THE EYES – HE HAD SQUARE EYES! AND HE SAID, 'LOOK, YOU PAY TUPPENCE A WEEK FOR FIFTY YEARS. THAT'S ALL. AND WHEN YOU GET TO NINETY, YOU GET A HUNDRED POUNDS. I KNOW IT'S NOT MUCH, BUT IT'S A GREAT START IN LIFE.'

TOMMY AT THE WHEEL

I call my car 'Flattery' – it gets me nowhere!

I just solved the parking problem – I bought a parked car!

We were bumper to bumper. I saw a fellow walking. I said, 'Would you like a lift?' He said, 'No thanks, I'm in a hurry.'

In order to go over ten miles an hour I have to remove the license plates from my car. It just won't pull that kind of a load!

I took a look at my tyres the other day. I've seen more rubber on the end of a pencil.

My new car has no clutch, no brake, no engine. There's only one trouble with it. They can't drive it out of the factory.

I don't feel so good. I got in late last night and I rammed right into my garage doors. I even knocked one off. It's a good thing I didn't have the car!

Someone actually complimented me on my driving the other day. They put a note on my windscreen that said, 'Parking fine.' So that was nice.

COOPER
CLASSIC
5

THIS LADY WENT TO THIS GREAT PAINTER AND SHE
SAID TO THE PAINTER, 'I'D LIKE A PORTRAIT DONE OF
MYSELF, A BIG ONE TO PUT IN MY HOUSE, SEE.' SHE
SAID, 'I'VE HEARD YOU'RE VERY GOOD. I DON'T WANT
YOU TO PUT ANY DIMPLES IN THAT AREN'T THERE.
DON'T DO THAT. I WANT YOU TO CAPTURE ME EXACTLY
AS I REALLY AM.' AND SHE SAID, 'IF YOU'VE GOT ANY
PAINT LEFT OVER,' SHE SAID, 'WOULD YOU PAINT A
DIAMOND AND RUBY NECKLACE ROUND MY THROAT LIKE
THAT. NOT LIKE THAT. LIKE THAT. AND DIAMOND AND
RUBY BRACELETS AND A DIAMOND AND RUBY RING AND
A BIG TIARA.' AND THE PAINTER SAID, 'THAT WILL BE
NO TROUBLE AT ALL.' HE SAID, 'BUT I'D LIKE TO KNOW
WHY ARE YOU DOING THAT?' SHE SAID, 'WELL, I'LL TELL
YOU WHAT, MY HUSBAND'S UP TO NO GOOD. AND WHEN
HE MARRIES HIS SECOND WIFE, SHE'S EITHER GOING
TO HAVE A NERVOUS BREAKDOWN OR DROP DOWN DEAD
LOOKING FOR THE NECKLACE AND THE BRACELETS.'
HUH HUH HUH!

COOPER BY ROYAL COMMAND

I'll never forget that Royal Variety Performance in the sixties. There I am standing in the line up on the stage of the London Palladium. They're all there. Jimmy Tarbuck, Cliff Richard, Lena Horne. And the Queen comes up to me. And she says, 'Oh, Mr. Cooper, you were really wonderful tonight, really you were.' And I went, 'Oh, thank you, ma'am. Did you laugh?' And she went, 'Oh yes, we all laughed.' And I said, 'That's good – then could I ask you something personal?' Well, the Queen, she looked at me – with her eyes – and she said, 'As personal as I'll allow.' And I said, 'Does your majesty like football?' She said, 'Not particularly.' And I said, 'Well, could I have your tickets for the Cup Final?'

THE HATS ROUTINE

No performance by Tommy Cooper was complete without his rendition of this classic routine, specially written by Val Andrews and Freddie Sadler soon after he became famous in the mid-fifties.

*In this classic routine Tommy stands beside
a table upon which rests a shabby cardboard
box. The box is full of hats, which he puts
on one at a time to illustrate the tale he has
to tell, returning each one to the box before
putting on the next, an inevitable blueprint
for confusion and chaos.*

I tell you what I'd like to do for you now if
I may - I'd like to recite for you a poem. It's
a love story - a sophisticated story along the
lines of Noël Coward, in which I shall play
every part and to clarify each character I play
I wear different hats. And the poem is called
'New Year's Eve.'

It was New Year's Eve in Joe's Pub, a happy
mob was there.

The bar and tables were
crowded, lots of noise
filled the air.

In the midst of all this
gaiety the door banged
open wide.

A torn and tattered
tramp walked in.

'Happy New Year, folks,'
he cried.

(Tommy puts on a floppy, felt Tramp's hat...)

The crowd just looked at him
and laughed and some began
to jeer,

*(He replaces Tramp's hat
with Sailor's hat...)*

But a sailor standing at the bar
said, 'Ship ahoy, mate, have
a beer.'

(Back to Tramp's hat...)

'I thank you, sir,' the
tramp replied, 'the beer
and me are through.

I'll never touch a drop
again, but I'll split a
bottle of rum with you.'

*(He now puts on a battered
old Bowler hat...)*

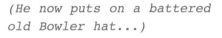

Then up jumped an old banker, who happened
to be there,

'Throw that tramp out,' he cried,
'he contaminates the air.'

(Back to Sailor's hat...)

'Them's harsh words, friend,'
the sailor said.

(Back to Bowler...)

The banker said,
'So what!'

*(Next a Cowboy's
Stetson...)*

'Them's shooting words,'
a cowboy said. 'Are you
aimin' to be shot?'

(At this point Tommy gets excited and forgets the words. To get back on track he has to return to the beginning for his own sake, reprising everything that has gone before sotto voce *and switching the hats around at a great pace until he catches up...)*

I won't be a minute.

(Eventually...)

Oh, yes!

(He puts on Soldier's hat...)

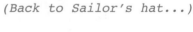

Then up jumped a soldier, who was standing at the bar,

'This ain't no time
to fight.'

(Back to Sailor's hat...)

'You're right,' said the
   sailor...

(The Bowler...)

And the banker said,
'Well, all right.'

Then up jumped a woman

*(He quickly produces
a lady's bonnet — a
hat that is funny in
itself...)*

And stared at the
tramp.

'My goodness, it's
Sam,' she cried with
fright and her face
went white.

(A Fireman's helmet...)

'Who's Sam?' a fireman asked,

(Tramp's hat...)

And the tramp pulled
out a knife and said:

'I am Sam', he cried,
'and that painted woman
once called herself my
wife.'

(Stetson...)

'Don't stand for it,'
the cowboy said.

(Soldier's hat...)

'Give me the knife,'
the soldier cried.

(Fireman's helmet...)

The fireman then hit the tramp

And said, 'That painted woman is my promised bride.'

(Tramp's hat...)

'Nuts, don't make me laugh,' the tramp replied,

'You cannot wed that horse.'

(Fireman's helmet...)

'Why not?' said the fireman.

(Tramp's hat...)

The tramp replied, 'We never were divorced.'

(Lady's bonnet...)

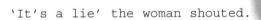

'It's a lie' the woman shouted.

(Tramp's hat...)

'It's the truth,' the tramp yelled out.

'Hold everything,' said the sailor,

(Tommy rummages for the Sailor's hat but can't immediately find it...)

I've got to get a bigger box! Where was I up to? Help me out. We're gonna be here all night! Oh - the sailor!

(The Sailor's hat...)

'Hold everything,' said the sailor,

'What the heck's it all about?'

(Bowler...)

'Who are you to but in?' the banker said.

(Stetson...)

The cowboy said, 'Shut up.'

(Soldier's hat...)

The soldier said, 'Hold it boys,'

And the fireman said...

(Tommy brings up the Fireman's helmet sharply and 'accidentally' hits himself with considerable force on the forehead. He registers pain and appeals to the wings...)

Now that is dangerous, that is. You should have padded that a bit. I could have cut my head open with that.

(He finishes putting on the helmet and resumes the poem...)

And the fireman said, 'I'll kill that pup.'

'Aaah...

(Searching again, he comes up with a Pilot's leather helmet...)

...A tough guy,' said the pilot...

(Tommy lifts the earflaps...)

I can't hear myself!

...Who was standing at the bar.

(Stetson...)

Then the cowboy hit the fireman,

(Fireman's helmet...)

And the fireman hit the floor.

He got up straightaway and looked at the woman and said, 'I was a mug for you to fall.'

And then he hit her.

'By gosh,' she screamed.

(Lady's bonnet...)

'Aaargh!'

And then the fight was free for all.

(Tight beret...)

In rushed a Frenchman.

(Cap...)

A little schoolboy.

(An Admiral's hat, which he slings to one side...)

I don't know who that is!

In the middle of all this fighting you could hear the knuckles crunch,

When all of a sudden they heard a policeman's whistle...

(No sound — he raises his voice...)

They heard a policeman's whistle...

(No sound — he raises his voice some more...)

They heard a policeman's whistle...

(At last we hear the sound of a whistle from the wings. Tommy surveys the stagehand with disdain...)

Isn't it marvellous, eh? That's all he has to do. And he's wearing make-up as well!

(He finally puts on a Policeman's helmet...)

And then a policeman came in and pinched the whole damn bunch!

Thank you very much. Goodnight!

A LAST ROUNDUP

JUST BEFORE THE SHOW THE PRODUCER TOOK ME TO ONE SIDE AND LEFT ME THERE! HE CAME BACK AND HE SAID, 'HOW DO YOU FEEL TONIGHT?' I SAID, 'A LITTLE BIT FUNNY.' HE SAID, 'WELL, GET OUT THERE BEFORE IT WEARS OFF.'

I MET THIS MAN AT THE AIRPORT. HE SAID, 'WOULD YOU LIKE TO SHARE A TAXI WITH ME?' I SAID, 'OKAY.' HE SAID, 'YOU TAKE THE WHEELS, I'LL TAKE THE ENGINE.'

THIS MAN SAT NEXT TO ME ON THE PLANE. HE SAID, 'I'VE GOT A PARROT AT HOME THAT SAYS, "WHO'S A PRETTY BOY, THEN? WHO'S A PRETTY BOY?"' I SAID, 'WELL, WHAT'S SO SPECIAL ABOUT THAT? A LOT OF PARROTS SAY, "WHO'S A PRETTY BOY? WHO'S A PRETTY BOY?"' HE SAID, 'YES, BUT THIS ONE'S STUFFED.'

OUR DOG WAS RUBBING TWO STICKS TOGETHER. MY LITTLE BOY SAID, 'WHAT'S HE TRYING TO TELL US, DAD?' I SAID, 'HE'S TRYING TO TELL US HE WANTS TO JOIN THE BOY SCOUTS!'

ONE KANGAROO SAID TO THE OTHER, 'I HOPE IT DOESN'T RAIN. I HATE IT WHEN THE KIDS HAVE TO PLAY INSIDE!'

THE OTHER WEEK I HAD TO SHARE MY DRESSING ROOM WITH A MONKEY. THE PRODUCER CAME IN AND SAID, 'I'M SORRY ABOUT THIS.' I SAID, 'THAT'S OKAY.' HE SAID, 'I WASN'T TALKING TO YOU.'

'BOOK, JOKE –
JOKE, BOOK!'

COMPILED BY JOHN FISHER

TOMMY COOPER
All In One Joke Book

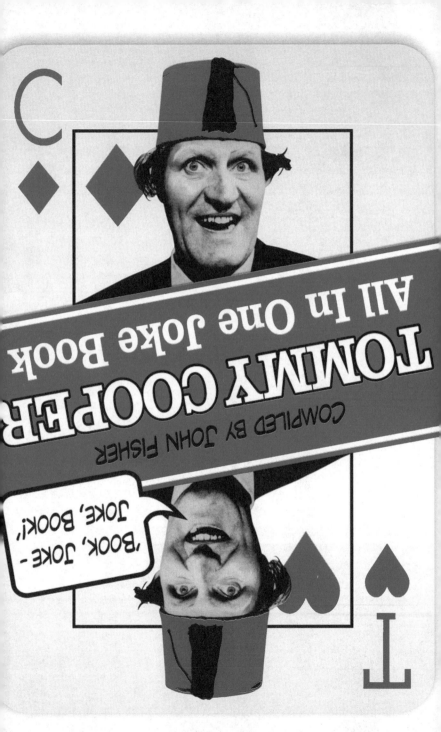

Acknowledgements

would like to thank Tommy's daughter, Vicky Cooper and John Miles, on behalf o
the Tommy Cooper Estate, for their support of this project.

Special acknowledgment is also made to Fred Allen, Val Andrews, Eddie Bayliss
ack Benny, Milton Berle, Martin Breese, Peter Cagney, Simon Callow, Gwen
Cooper, David Drummond, Pinkie DuFort, Beatrice Ferrie, Miff Ferrie, Jerome Flynn
Colin Fox, the team at FremantleMedia, Eddie Gay, Billy Glason, Tommy Godfrey,
Buddy Hackett, Vince Healy, David Hemingway, Sir Anthony Hopkins, Peter Hudson
udor Jones and the members of the Tommy Cooper Appreciation Society, Gershon
egman, Henry Lewis, Trevor Lewis, Clive Mantle, Jay Marshall, Max Miller, Si
Spike Milligan, Bob Monkhouse, Robert Orben, Art Paul, Patrick Ryecart, Freddie
Sadler, Stuart Snaith and the team at 2entertain, Jerry Seinfeld, Eric Sykes, Chris
Woodward and Henny Youngman.

revor Dolby, at Preface, had the foresight to see how Tommy Cooper could
nake us laugh again on the printed page and I extend my thanks to him and his
eam including Nicola Taplin, Katherine Murphy and Neil Bradford. While every
effort has been made to trace the owners of copyright material produced herein
he publishers would like to apologise for any omissions and will be pleased to
ncorporate missing acknowledgments in future editions, provided that notification
s made to them in writing.

Andy Spence took on the challenge of committing the range and detail of the Coope
oke archive to the printed page. Coupled with my thanks to him is the wish that m
comic hero could have seen the results of his research arranged so accessibly. As
always, I also owe a major debt of gratitude to my representative, Charles Armitage
and his associate Di Evans. The loving support of my wife Sue does without saying

IER MONTHLY

COMEDIAN"

SSIONAL COMEDY MATERIAL
of the DAY-WEEK-MONTH

SERVICE OF THE STARS"
MONTHLY SERVICE"
.....ighted by

ISSUE #150
6th issue
13th year

GAY'S GAGS
242 West 72nd St.
New York 23, N.Y.

PER YEAR   MARCH 1961   ISS

TERIAL WRITTEN BY EDDIE GAY

THE ENTERTAINER
242 West 72nd Street
New York City
SU 7-4068

$10 per year   March 1959   Issue No. 3

IGINAL MATERIAL WRITTEN BY EDDIE GAY

f my left foot---that's why I ke
y swing---later he
n having trouble
Khrushchev.....My
ral person---excep
wo handicap---my s
y tough lies I tho
er and my last was
course than there w
ly I've been getti
s after he gets in
were faster than S
The 14th wa

20

FUN-MASTER

(Title Reg. U. S. Patent Office)

GAG FILE No. 20

Compiled by Billy Glason

STORIES

flyer came to America for a visit on a ve
d a friend about America's
of our co

ONTHLY

LAN"

MEDY MATERIAL
Y-WEEK-MONTH

HE STARS"
ERVICE"
.....ighted by
N
ty, 19, N.Y.
ISSUES $3
ISSUES $4
FUNDS)
SON

ISSUE
#149

RFORMING RIGHTS ONLY

ISSUE #149
5th issue
13th year

MONTHLY

COMEDIAN"

SIONAL COMEDY MATERIAL consisting
a DAY, WEEK and MONTH

ished by
GLASON'S FUN-MASTER
Street, New York City, 19, New York
mittances payable to BILLY GLASON
SCRIPTION: $15 pr year

APRIL
1955

LIST OF CONTENTS

AIES.........
-LINE.......

#

FUN-MASTER GAG FILE #24
(Title Reg. U. S. Patent Office)
Compiled by Billy Glason

ride on his new motorcycle. After they had gone a f
it. "Shure and it's fine", said Mike, "But th
the side of the road and said: "Turn yo
t shud protect your chest". a
k. When the constable sa
dead. This man h
wisted his

Zebras

A leopard went to see a psychiatrist. He said, 'Every time I look at my wife I see spots before my eyes.' The psychiatrist said, 'That's only natural.' The leopard said, 'But doctor, she's a zebra!'

A man went to see a psychiatrist. He said, 'It's odd, but I feel that I'm a zebra. Everywhere I look on my body I see black stripes.' The psychiatrist said, 'Take one of these pills every day for a week and it should get rid of the black stripes.' He came back in a few days and said, 'Doctor, I feel great. The black stripes have gone. Have you anything for the white ones?'

The zebra said to the lion, 'Let's switch roles for a while.' The lion said, 'Okay, I'm game!'

Zoo

Two leopards were being fed at the zoo. One sat back and said, 'That hit just the right spot!'

This big elephant and this tiny mouse were in the same cage at the zoo. The elephant was in a really foul mood. He looked down at the mouse and said, 'You are the weakest, puniest, most insignificant creature I've ever seen.' The mouse said, 'But don't forget ... I've been ill!'

I went to the zoo the other day and the zoo-keeper started chasing me because I was feeding the monkeys. I was feeding them to the lions!

This fellow worked at the zoo throwing fish to the pelicans. It wasn't a great job, but it filled the bill!

I took my wife to the zoo, but they wouldn't accept her!

Z is for Zebra

Y is for ...

Youth

I'll never forget my first girlfriend. Her father shot at me, her brother threw stones at me and her mother hit me with a broom. I can take a hint!

When I was young I always leaned towards blondes ... but they kept pushing me back!

Youth is the first forty years of your life, but the first twenty of everybody else's!

In the words of Milton Berle, 'We spend the first half of our lives trying to understand the older generation, and the second half trying to understand the younger!'

In other words, if young people were wise, they'd miss half the fun!

Adolescence is when boys begin to notice that girls notice boys who notice girls.

I'll never forget my first sweetheart. I asked her father if I could marry her. Her father said, 'Can you make her happy?' I said, 'Happy? You should have seen her last night in the back of the car!'

It wasn't easy to get us kids to eat olives. I had to start off on martinis!

A woman should hold on to her youth, but not when she's driving!

Y is for Youth

X

Have you ever thought ... if you sign something with an 'X', how do you cross it out?

I've invented a new cleaning fluid. It gets rid of all the Xs that mark the spot!

X-Rated

I saw my first X-rated Western the other day. Even the wagons weren't covered!

X-Rays

I gave her an X-ray of my chest. I just wanted to show her my heart was in the right place!

My doctor is an old-fashioned doctor. He doesn't give you an X-ray ... he just holds you up to the light!

A hospital technician got married to a woman who'd come in for an X-ray ... he must have seen something in her!

I said to the consultant, 'My head feels like there are a million little teeny-weeny light bulbs in there.' He said, 'Why don't you have it X-rayed?' I said, 'I did.' He said, 'What did they find?' I said, 'A million little teeny-weeny light bulbs!'

Xylophone

Two dinosaurs walked passed a xylophone. One of them said, 'She's pretty, but she's all skin and bones!'

"THE COMEDIAN" for JAN
Vol.9 No.6 (102nd iss

<u>M O R E   O N E - L I N E R S</u> (continue

He wasn't bald, his head just grew up through hi

My act got a wonderful review--in "POPULAR MECHA

My golf is sure improving. I'm missing the ball
than I used to.

It isn't the line you GIVE a gal that BOTHERS her
PAWS in between!

I don't know where my next dollar's coming from b
already knows where it's going!

She's always making mountains out of moth-balls!

When I was born I was so fat my Mother had to jack
change my diapers! (or: when HE was born, etc.)

I gave my girl a cultured pearl set--a dozen oyster

Boy, was that restaurant expensive! I said to the
"Haven't you got any slightly used steaks?"

Before I leave I have some advice for you people wh
falling asleep. Drink a pint of rye before you
<u>S L E E P   T I G H T!</u>

I got a one-man dog...he only bites ME!

Every time he gets a raise his wife gets a new hat.
seems to go to HER head!

You can always cure your husband's snoring by kindnes
advice, friendly cooperation--and by STUFFING AN
IN HIS MOUTH!

X is for

W
X

Women

When meeting a beautiful girl an Englishman raises an eyebrow, a Frenchman kisses her hand, an American asks for her phone number and a Russian cables the Kremlin for instructions!

She's the kind of woman, if she can't say anything good about another woman, she loves it!

She was so beautiful, when I took her home in a taxi, I could hardly keep my eyes on the meter!

I'm fussy what kind of girl I go out with ... they've got to have shoes!

She was wearing a living bra ... and it bit her!

She's a Cinderella girl ... at the stroke of twelve, she passes out!

She's the kind of girl you look at twice. The first time you don't believe it!

Since she left me I can't sleep a wink ... she took the mattress with her!

Worry

I offered a guy a hundred pounds to worry for me. He said, 'Where's the hundred quid?' I said, 'That's your first worry!'

Wrestling

I used to be a wrestler. You know, some wrestlers wear a toga ... some wear a leopard skin ... and some wear fancy robes. Me – I was different. I wore a suit of armour!

I used to be an all-in wrestler. I had to give it up. After the first round I was all in!

My wife ran away with the gardener. Isn't that awful? Good gardeners are hard to find!

After we were married she told me she would cook and darn all my socks. I said, 'That won't be necessary ... just darn them!'

My wife is a magician. Yesterday she turned our car into a tree!

My wife's got a heart of gold ... hard and yellow!

My wife's a light eater ... as soon as it gets light she starts eating!

My wife couldn't close her eyes all night. She put her eyelashes on backwards!

She said, 'Do you like my hair in a bun?' I said, 'I wouldn't care if you wore it in a loaf of bread!'

My wife does great bird impressions – she watches me like a hawk!

I said, 'But if you saw someone stealing our car, why didn't you scream or something?' She said, 'Don't worry. I wrote down the registration number before he got out of sight!'

The other day my wife asked me for fifty pounds. I said, 'Money, money, money ... that's all you ever ask me for is money! You need brains instead of money.' She said, 'Maybe, but I just thought I'd ask you for what you had the most of!'

She never argues. She just tells me I'm wrong and lets it go at that.

Mind you – I always get the last word. I apologise!

I won't say what kind of driver she is, but once she was hit by a house!

She once got a speeding ticket going through the car wash!

Once she left the garage at fifty miles an hour and then came back ... she forgot the car!

One day my wife came home with the car a total wreck. I said, 'What happened?' She said, 'Well, it was either run into this other car or else have an accident!'

When she was brought into court, the judge said it was the worst case of hit-and-run he had ever seen. He thought she was the victim!

I don't know what to buy my wife for her birthday. I don't know whether to buy her a box of chocolates, a diamond ring, a fur coat or a new car. That's what I'll get her ... a box of chocolates.

I asked the girl behind the counter what can I get for my wife? She said, 'I don't know. What are you asking for her?'

My wife is always telling me that women are like wine ... the older they get, the better they become. So I locked her in the cellar!

At least when she drives, people are safe on the street ... she drives on the pavement!

I said to my wife, 'Why don't you stop at red lights?' She said, 'Once you've seen one, you've seen them all!'

My wife phoned. She said, 'There's water in the carburettor.' I said, 'Where's the car?' She said, 'In the lake!'

She always serves me food that melts in the mouth, but how many ice cubes can a man swallow?

Actually she bakes wonderfully – on the beach!

You know why I call her 'Dear' ... she's got antlers sticking out of her head!

There's only one place I go when I want to get away from her. I hide in the kitchen!

She cooks so bad, the cat has only three lives left!

The other day I asked her when she was going to straighten up the house. She said, 'Why? Is it tilted?'

One day I asked her why my shaving brush was as stiff as a board. She said, 'I don't know ... it felt soft yesterday, when I was painting the birdcage!'

She's the kind of wife – when she can't find any hairs on your coat, she accuses you of running around with a bald-headed woman!

I said, 'Why do you wear your wedding ring on the wrong finger?' She said, 'Because I married the wrong guy!'

She just got her driver's licence. Now all her accidents will be legal. What she doesn't know about driving a car would fill a hospital!

To give you an idea of how my wife drives, the other day she almost killed me backing out of the garage. She said, 'Thank goodness it was only you. It might have been a stranger!'

W
X

My wife and I used to have such fun at the beach. First she would bury me in the sand, then I would bury her in the sand. One of these days I'm going to go back and dig her up!

I took my wife out to lunch. Halfway through the meal she fainted. The waiter rushed up and said, 'Do you want a stretcher?' I said, 'No, thank you. She's long enough as she is!'

She keeps asking me for something to drive. So I bought her a hammer and a packet of nails!

Everything Sophia Loren wears my wife goes out and buys. The other day she bought a pair of those Italian sandals and now she looks just like her ... from the ankles down!

Take away Sophia Loren's sexy look and take away her figure and what have you got? My wife!

She's the best little wife a guy ever had ... even if her husband doesn't think so!

They say a woman's work is never done and my wife's cooking proves it!

My wife is the fussiest housekeeper you ever saw. She even puts a newspaper under the cuckoo clock!

She's always complaining about clothes. The other day she said, 'Just look at me. My clothes are so shabby. If anyone came to the door they'd think I was the cook.' I said, 'Not if they stayed to dinner!'

She has been trying to keep up with the Joneses for years and we finally made it. We now owe as much money as they do!

My wife is one of those women who always enters a room voice first!

She's got me where I eat out of her hand ... saves a lot of dishwashing!

I've got a wife who never misses me. Her aim is perfect!

My wife decided to knit me a pair of socks. They're fine, but just a little snug under the arms!

I found a way to cure my wife from falling out of bed. I make her sleep on the floor!

She is always complaining about headaches, but it's her own fault. I keep telling her – if she's going to jump out of bed, she should do it feet first!

I can't stand my wife smoking in bed. I know a lot of women smoke in bed, but face down?

I said to my wife, 'Let's go out tonight and have some fun.' She said, 'Okay, but leave the hall light on if you get in before me!'

One day I came home and found a big cake with seven candles on it. I said, 'Whose birthday is it?' She said, 'That's for the dress I'm wearing ... it's seven years old today!'

Actually I take my wife everywhere, but she keeps coming back!

I met my wife at a dance ... I thought she was at home with the kids!

W
X

My wife dislocated her jaw and couldn't talk. So I phoned the doctor and told him to drop round anytime in a few weeks or a month!

My wife and I were having lunch together and she said, 'Would you pass me over the mustard!' So I did ... she wasn't half heavy!

I'm a little worried about her tonight. This morning she left home at nine o'clock and she isn't back yet. I don't know what to think. She may have gone shopping or she may have been in an accident or kidnapped or even murdered. Gee, I hope she isn't shopping!

I don't like to talk about my wife behind her back. I only do it because it's safer that way!

I'm not knocking my wife. She is kind and considerate and really too good for me. If only she'd realise this and leave me!

She's such a terrible cook, for ten years she thought poached eggs were illegal!

My wife had a bad habit of biting her nails, but I cured her. I hid her teeth!

I bought my wife a mink stole and now I'm up to her neck in debt!

I'm the boss in my family. Every night when I get home my wife brings me my slippers, my pipe and my apron!

My wife said, 'Why don't you buy me a mink coat? I'm always cold.' I said, 'That's why!'

My wife's a lovely mover ... she works for Pickfords!

The other night I had an argument with my wife in the launderette ... but we went home and ironed things out!

My wife is the kind of wife who when she has a bad night wakes her husband and says, 'What's the matter? Can't you sleep either?'

Wives

I asked my wife to marry me and be the mother of my children. She said, 'How many have you got?'

I'll never forget the first time I took her home to meet my mother. I said, 'This girl is just wonderful. She loves to cook. She loves to sew. She takes care of the house and does everything.' My mother said, 'That's good. I'll use her on Tuesdays and Thursdays!'

When I first met my wife, every morning I tried to bring her breakfast in bed. It wasn't easy ... she lived at the YWCA.

My wife and I never quarrel. You know why? I'm a coward!

I gave my wife a ring on her birthday. I reversed the charges!

There was a guy sitting there holding a piece of rope up in the air. I said, 'What's that for?' He said, 'This is a weather gauge.' I said, 'How can you predict the weather with a piece of rope?' He said, 'It's easy. When the rope swings back and forth, it's windy and when it gets wet, it's raining!'

It was ninety in the shade. I'm no fool – I stayed in the sun!

Weddings

The other day I went to a wedding and I never saw two happier people. Not the bride and groom – her parents!

Was the bride jealous! She was the only bride who ever had a male bridesmaid!

A wedding is a funeral where you smell your own flowers!

I'll never forget our wedding. Her mother cried and her father cried. I never saw two people cry so much. No wonder ... it cost a fortune!

The trouble with being best man at a wedding ... you never get a chance to prove it!

I had a brass band at our wedding. I put it on my wife's finger!

Well Dressed

See Introduction: page 11

What If?

What if William Tell had been nearsighted?

What if Abraham Lincoln had waited to see it on TV?

What if Lady Godiva had had a crew cut?

I said, 'How long will my spaghetti be?' The waiter said, 'I don't know ... we never measure it!'

He said, 'Do you want red or white?' I said, 'I don't mind. I'm colour-blind.'

I thought I'd start a conversation, so I said to the waiter, 'It looks like rain.' He said, 'I know, but it's soup!'

Wand

Here's a magic wand ... there's a white tip there and a white tip there ... now the reason for the white tips is to separate the ends from the centre!

Weather

It was so cold, my teeth were chattering so much, I couldn't put them back in my mouth!

It was so cold, my teeth were chattering so much, they broke the glass I keep them in!

It was so cold, my teeth were chattering so much, I took them out and went to bed!

It was so cold, I opened my wardrobe door and my best suit was wearing my overcoat!

I went to Margate for my holidays. It was so cold. There was a guy shivering on the beach in a bathing suit. He was purple all over. I said, 'You can't expect to get a tan in this weather.' He said, 'Well, I'm going home with some colour and I don't care what colour it is!'

The waiter gave me a menu. It had everything on it, so I asked for a clean one!

I said to the waiter, 'A piece of plaster just fell in my soup.' He said, 'Well, as long as you're paying ceiling prices, you're entitled to a piece of the ceiling!'

This fellow had rice in his hair. I said, 'Did you get married today?' He said, 'No, I had a fight with a Chinese waiter!'

I said, 'Waiter, this chicken's got one leg shorter than the other.' He said, 'What do you want to do? Eat it or dance with it?'

Last night I ordered a whole meal in French. The waiter was surprised. It was a Chinese restaurant!

The waiter brought me everything but a spoon. I said, 'This coffee is too hot for me to stir with my finger!' He brought me another cup and said, 'This one's a lot cooler!'

I said to the waiter, 'There's no chicken in this chicken soup.' He said, 'And there's no horse in the horseradish either!'

When I go to a restaurant I like my food hot. So I told the waiter I wanted my soup real hot. I said, 'I mean it should be real boiling hot. In fact, if you can carry it, don't bother bringing it because it won't be hot enough!'

A cannibal boarded a cruise ship and went to the dining room. The waiter said, 'Menu, sir?' He said, 'No, the passenger list!'

I said to the waiter, 'How do you get a glass of water in this place?' He said, 'I don't know ... how about setting yourself on fire?'

Waiters

A waiter is a man who believes that money grows on trays!

One day a waiter fell sick and was rushed to hospital. He was lying on the table in great pain when a doctor passed by. He said, 'Hey doctor, can't you do something for me?' The doctor said, 'I'm sorry. This isn't my table!'

The waiters at my hotel ... they're so sentimental. One of them held out his hand and said, 'I hope you're not going to forget me.' I shook his hand and said, 'Of course not. I'll write every day!'

I went into a restaurant and waited an hour to be served. Eventually I grabbed a waiter and said, 'How about something to eat?' He said, 'Who's got time to sit down?'

I said to the waiter, 'There's a fly in my soup.' He said, 'I know ... the chef used to be a tailor!'

I said, 'Do you serve shepherd's pie?' He said, 'Of course, as long as they leave their sheep outside!'

I said to the waiter, 'Hey, what kind of duck is this? It tastes like fish.' He said, 'I know. It's haddock!'

I found a fly in my soup and said to the waiter, 'What's the meaning of this?' He said, 'How should I know. I'm a waiter, not a fortune teller!'

I said to the waiter, 'There's a fly in my ice cream.' He said, 'Serves him right ... let him freeze to death. This morning he was in the soup!'

W is for Wand

Value

There's an easy way of finding out the value of money ... try to borrow some!

Vegetables

Every day this guy came into a bar with a potato stuck in his ear. Then one day he showed up with a stick of celery in his ear instead. The barman said, 'Why the change?' He said, 'The doctor told me to cut out fattening foods!'

Vegetarian

My little boy bit into an apple, saw a worm and said, 'From now on I'll think I'll be a vegetarian!'

Ventriloquists

This ventriloquist fell on hard times and was forced to take work as the accomplice of a phoney medium. At one séance he was pretending to be Mr Smith, whose widow had paid fifty pounds for the privilege. After talking to her husband for a long time, she said, 'I can't believe I could talk to my husband for just fifty pounds.' The ventriloquist said, 'Well, for a hundred you could talk to him while he's drinking a glass of water!'

This fellow walked into a bar with a chicken under one arm and a crocodile under the other. The barman said, 'What'll you have?' He said, 'A whiskey and soda.' Then the crocodile spoke up and said, 'I'll have a gin and tonic.' The barman said, 'That's amazing. I've never seen a crocodile that could talk before.' He said, 'He can't. The chicken's a ventriloquist!'

Violin

I play the violin just like Menuhin ... under the chin!

V is for Ventriloquist

Ugly

In school I had to stand with my face to the wall ... not because I was bad, but because I was ugly!

She was so ugly, she kept sending her mirror back for repairs!

She was too ugly to have her face lifted, so they lowered her body instead!

Umbrella

Let a smile be your umbrella ... and you'll get soaking wet!

Yesterday I saw five men standing under a single umbrella and not one of them got a drop of water on him. It wasn't raining!

Undertakers

Never trust an undertaker ... he'll always let you down!

I said, 'You told me your son was a doctor.' He said, 'No I didn't ... I said he followed the medical profession!'

This undertaker was complaining about business. He said, 'I haven't buried a living soul for three months!'

This fellow phoned an undertaker to sort out his wife's funeral. The undertaker said, 'Your wife? Didn't I bury her two years ago?' He said, 'I married again.' The undertaker said, 'Congratulations!'

This girl started to date an undertaker. Her friend said, 'You should be careful. He may be after you for your body!'

U is for Umbrella

Transport

I feel travel sick. I just got off a train and had to ride backwards all the way. Someone said, 'Why didn't you ask somebody sitting opposite to change seats with you?' I said, 'I would have, but I was all alone in the carriage!"

A man was standing next to me on the bus when he tapped me on the shoulder. He said, 'Are you getting off soon?' I said, 'No. Why?' He said, 'You're standing on my foot!'

Travel

I've been to Paris so many times I'm beginning to feel like a parasite!

We went to Switzerland and there was this beautiful mountain. I said to the guide, 'There must be romantic stories about it.' He said, 'Yes. One day two lovers climbed to the top and they were never seen again.' I said, 'What happened?' He said, 'They went down the other side!'

I took my wife on a cruise and she threw the laundry out of the porthole. She thought it was a washing machine.

When I was in Paris I spent two days in my room trying to learn enough French to get downstairs!

S
T

Tunnel

The British and the French were discussing the Channel Tunnel. The chief engineer said, 'The idea is that we'll send a thousand men in one end and a thousand men in the other end and they'll meet halfway.' Someone said, 'But suppose they don't meet.' The engineer said, 'Then we'll have two tunnels!'

Things always turn out right in the end. I knew an old man who was unlucky all his life. Then when they were digging his grave they struck oil.

Never tell people your troubles. Half of them are not interested and the other half are glad you're getting what's coming to you!

And never worry about getting older. Just remember that when you stop getting older, you're dead!

Tips

To show my appreciation I gave the decorator an extra ten pounds and told him to take the missus to the movies. That night he was back wearing his best clothes. I said, 'What's the matter? Did you forget something?' He said, 'No, I just came back to take the missus to the movies.'

Town

As Fred Allen said, the town was so dull one day the tide went out and it never came back!

Traffic

The traffic is so bad. One day I was offered a lift and said, 'No thanks ... I'm in a hurry!'

Tramp

A tramp asked me if I could give him something for a cup of coffee ... so I gave him a lump of sugar!

Show me a man who lost all his money and can still laugh and I'll show you an idiot!

You haven't a real hangover until you can't stand the noise made by Alka Seltzer!

As my father used to say, 'Never cry over spilt milk ... it could have been whiskey!'

Love your enemies ... it'll drive them nuts!

A barking dog never whistles!

My mind keeps saying I shouldn't drink and have anything to do with women. The rest of me says, 'Who asked you?'

Why is it you always see a parking space when you haven't got a car?

In the words of that great philosopher, 'A friend in need is a pest!'

If I had to live my life all over again ... I wouldn't have the strength!

When you lend a friend ten pounds and you never see him again ... it's worth it!

S
T

Where did mothers learn all those things they tell their daughters not to do?

There's only one thing to give a man who has everything ... penicillin!

You can lead a horse to water, but teach him to lie on his back and float and you've got something!

Teeth

I could tell she had false teeth ... it came out in conversation!

Forgive me if I speak slowly ... I lost my bridge on the River Kwai!

Telephone

My wife answered the phone, said, 'Yes, that's right,' and put it down again. I said, 'Who was that?' She said, 'It's some woman who keeps saying "Long distance from America"!'

One thing worries me ... why aren't wrong numbers ever busy?

Television

My wife watches so many medical shows, I can only talk to her during visiting hours!

I'm in favour of pay television ... if they pay me, I'll watch anything!

Television has opened up a whole new field of unemployment for me!

I always had trouble getting on television. I even offered to kill myself on TV. It would be a real first!

Thoughts for the Day

I now leave you with a thought for the day ...

Everybody makes mistakes. An architect covers his mistakes with ivy, a doctor covers his mistakes with earth and a chef covers his mistakes with mayonnaise!

Tap

My little boy ... no one could do anything with him. His teacher said, 'What's the answer to water on the brain?' He said, 'A tap on the head!'

Tattoos

This tattooist wanted to draw a great big eagle right across his back. He always wanted to do it ... draw a great big eagle with a wing on each shoulder and its talons in the small of his back. For twenty years he wanted to do it, but he was so busy he couldn't get round to it!

Taxis

The taxi driver said, 'I'll charge two pounds each for you and your wife. The kids can ride for free.' The father turned to the kids and said, 'Okay. Jump in, children, and have a nice ride. Your mother and I will see you back at the hotel!'

I said to the driver, 'Can't you go any faster?' He said, 'I sure can, but I'm not allowed to leave the cab!'

A cab driver turned to his passenger and said, 'I couldn't help noticing that hearing aid you're wearing. Do you mind it much?' The passenger said, 'Not at all. As a matter of fact, nearly all of us have some physical weakness.' The driver said, 'You're right. Look at me. I can hardly see a foot in front of me!'

I know a cab driver who weighs 200 lbs, is six feet tall, chews tobacco and loves to fight. Even her husband is afraid of her!

T is for Tap

Strikes

Two guys were in a picket line. One of them said, 'Do you know what it's all about?' The other said, 'We're striking for shorter hours.' The other one said, 'I'm in favour of that. I always thought sixty minutes was too long!'

During the transport strike I saw an old lady standing by the side of the road and decided to give her a lift. After several miles I turned to her and said, 'Madam, where shall I let you out?' She said, 'Thank you, but I didn't want to say anything to hurt your feelings. I was going the other way!'

Superstition

I'm so superstitious, I wouldn't walk under a black cat!

Swimming

I tried to swim the Channel once, but I used too much grease. I kept slipping out of the water!

They always say start at the bottom if you want to learn something ... but suppose you want to learn to swim?

A lifeguard on the beach heard a man yelling for help. He shouted, 'Help! I can't swim. I've got my hands in my pockets. Help!' The lifeguard picked up his megaphone and yelled back, 'Take your hands out of your pockets!' The man yelled back, 'What ... and let the water in?'

They've got a big sign that says, 'No Smoking In The Pool.' Are they afraid the water will catch fire?

S
T

My doctor told me to stay away from cigarettes and to try chocolate bars instead. I did, but I had trouble keeping them alight.

I said to the doctor, 'I'm worried about my wife smoking.' He said, 'But a lot of women smoke.' I said, 'I know, but she inhales.' He said, 'That's alright. A lot of women who smoke inhale.' I said, 'But she never exhales!'

If you want to stop smoking, carry wet matches!

Snooker

Did you hear about the snooker player who had a nervous breakdown? Every time he leaned over the table he got the shakes. His doctor prescribed a long rest!

Spring

Spring must be here ... this morning I heard the first robin coughing its little brains out!

Stardom

What a reception I got when I stepped off the plane. Everybody started shouting, 'There's Tony Curtis! There's Tony Curtis!' So I turned around and there was Tony Curtis!

Smoking

I got a beautiful smoking jacket for Christmas, but no matter how hard I stuff it into my pipe the sleeves still hang out!

I'm worried about my uncle ... he chews tobacco and then blows smoke rings!

The first time my wife saw me cut off the end of a cigar she said, 'Why don't you buy them the right size?'

This fellow said, 'I get dizzy spells from cigarettes.' I said, 'From inhaling them?' He said, 'No – from bending down to pick them up!'

S
T

When I sing, I sing with my heart and soul. I'll even sound better when I start using my voice!

When I sing, I cry. I cry because I can't sing!

(sung) He flew through the air with the greatest of ease ...
(spoken) ... he forgot his trapeze!

Sleep

Last night I slept like a log. I woke up in the fireplace!

I sleep like a baby. Every morning I wake up screaming around two!

I am so tired ... I don't know why. I had eight hours sleep last night. I think I must have slept slower than usual!

I worried that as soon as I get into bed I'll drop off ... I'd better order a bigger bed!

I was out all morning trying to get something for my wife ... and I couldn't get a single offer!

I went into this shop and said, 'Have you got a couple of nice steaks?' The guy behind the counter said, 'A couple of nice steaks?' I said, 'Yes – are they rare?' He said, 'Rare? In here they're impossible! You're in the chemist's!'

A cannibal went into a butcher's shop. He said, 'I'll have a pound and a half of Kate and Sidney!'

Two shopkeepers were discussing the drop in business. One said, 'Here it is ... June already and business is terrible.' The other said, 'Well, it's always this way before Christmas!'

Show Business

I've got show business in my blood ... I was bitten by an actor!

I got into show business because I couldn't find my regular line of work ... I'm a shepherd!

One day a guy came up to me and said, 'Hey, Mr Cooper, I want you to know that you're number one on my hit parade' ... so he hit me!

Shyness

I'm so shy, I can't take a bath unless I blindfold my rubber duck!

Singing

I've been taking singing lessons through the mail. I'll admit they haven't helped, but my postman sings like Sinatra!

Lots of people have said I have a voice like Caruso ... Robinson Caruso!

S
T

Shoes

My wife complained that her feet hurt. I said, 'You've got your shoes on the wrong feet.' She said, 'But these are the only feet I've got.'

I asked the manager if he had any loafers. He said, 'Just a minute and I'll get one of them to serve you!'

I saw an old tramp walking down the street wearing one shoe. I said, 'Hey, you lost your shoe.' He said, 'No, I found one!'

These shoes are killing me. They're so tight, my big toe and my little toe are now going steady!

Shopping

I went into a hardware store and asked the girl to show me some cheap skates. She said, 'I'm sorry, but both the owners are in Florida!'

I wanted to buy her some alligator shoes for her birthday, but I didn't know what size her alligator wore!

I went window shopping ... I couldn't find a window my size!

It isn't the wolf at the door that keeps some husbands broke. It's the mink in the window!

The other day my wife went down to the corner market ... she bought three corners!

I said, 'Do you stock sealing wax?' The girl said, 'I know we have floor wax, but I don't think we've anything for waxing a ceiling!'

Savings

Every day for two years I've been putting something aside for a rainy day, but what am I going to do with 500 umbrellas and 200 pairs of wellingtons?

Saw

He said, 'What kind of tricks do you do?' I said, 'You've heard of sawing a woman in half?' He said, 'Yes, but that trick's been around for years.' I said, 'Lengthwise?'

Scout

The scoutmaster asked three boy scouts if they had done their good deed for the day. They said, 'Yes, we helped an old lady across the road.' He said, 'Did it take all three of you to do that?' They said, 'Yes! She didn't want to go!'

Shakespeare

I've only read two of Shakespeare's plays – Romeo and Juliet!

I said, 'I've just written a play called *Hamlet*.' He said, '*Hamlet*? But Shakespeare wrote that hundreds of years ago.' I said, 'That's funny. They said the same when I wrote *Othello*!'

S is for Scout

A young girl came to a fancy dress party without any clothes on. The fellow at the door said, 'I'm sorry, miss, but this is a fancy dress party. You're supposed to be in costume and represent something.' So she left and came back later, still in the nude, but this time she was wearing a pair of black shoes and black gloves. The doorman said, 'And what are you supposed to represent?' She said, 'The five of spades!'

When I go out with my girl friend in the evening, she always wears an evening gown. When we go swimming, she wears a swimsuit and when we play tennis, she wears a tennis outfit. Now she won't talk to me. Just because I told her I was coming over to see her on her birthday!

A man went to court for a divorce. The judge asked him why he wanted a divorce and he said, 'Because my wife called me an idiot.' The judge said, 'That's hardly grounds for divorce. Why did she call you an idiot?' I said, 'Well, I came home early one day and caught her making love to another man, so I said, "Hey, what's going on here?" and she said, "Idiot!"'

A little girl was telling her kindergarten teacher, 'Me slept with daddy last night.' The teacher said, 'No, Mary, that's wrong. I slept with daddy last night.' The little girl said, 'Well then, you must have come in after I went to sleep.'

Q
R

Robbery

My neighbour called me the other day and said, 'Are you watching TV?' I said, 'No.' He said, 'I'm not surprised. A guy just came through your kitchen window carrying it!'

Romance

She said, 'Take me in your arms and whisper something soft and sweet.' I said, 'Chocolate fudge!'

said, 'A coyote.' I said, 'That's right. You're the first one to guess it.' He said, 'But what's with the cement?' I said, 'I just put that in to make it harder!'

Risqué

An eighty-year-old man married a twenty-year-old girl. One of his friends said, 'Let me give you some advice. If you want a happy marriage, take in a lodger.' A few months later they met up again. The friend said, 'How are things working out?' He said, 'They couldn't be better and I owe it all to your advice. What is more, my wife is pregnant.' The friend said, 'And how is the lodger?' He said, 'Oh, she's pregnant too!'

I saw an ad in the paper that read, 'For sale – valuable spot in the country with beautiful view overlooking nudist colony. Reason for moving – failing eyesight!'

This little boy was getting into a lot of trouble at school. His teacher told his mother he was annoying all the little girls and the mother said, 'Just like his father.' Then the teacher said, 'And he gets the little girls in a corner and hugs them and kisses them.' The mother said, 'Yes! Just like his father.' The teacher went on, 'In fact, he never leaves the girls alone ... he's after them all the time.' The mother said, 'Just like his father ... it's a good thing I didn't marry him!'

A woman called her butler into her bedroom and said, 'James, take off my dress. Now take off my slip and my brassiere. Now take off my stockings. Now don't ever let me catch you wearing my clothes again!'

I had a terrible dream the other night. I dreamt I was shipwrecked on a desert island with Jayne Mansfield and Diana Dors. That might not sound so bad, but I was Ava Gardner!

tried to make me eat chicken pie. Now I'm asking you, may I have the roast beef?' The manager turned to the head waiter and said, 'Throw this idiot out. He didn't come here to eat, he just came to argue!'

The portions they give you now are ridiculous. The other day a waiter came up and said, 'How did you find the steak?' I said, 'Oh, it was easy. I just lifted up a pea and there it was!'

I was in Paris with my wife and we were in this restaurant. Eventually I grabbed the waiter and said, 'Look here, garçon, my wife and I have been waiting to be served for over an hour. Will you please bring us a bottle of your best champagne?' He said, 'Oui, Monsieur. What year?' I said, 'Right now!'

I said to this Chinese waiter, 'Tell me something. Are there any Chinese Jews?' He said, 'I don't know. I'll go and find out.' So he went and he came back. He said, 'Sorry. There's only apple juice, orange juice and pineapple juice!'

I said, 'Have you got a game pie?' The waiter said, 'We certainly have ... it's fought its way out of the oven twice!'

Show me a man who comes home in the evening and is greeted with a smile, encouraged to take off his shoes, has pillows arranged all around him on the floor and is then served a delicious meal, and I'll show you a man who lives in a Japanese restaurant!

The food was on the table ... but I insisted on plates!

I said to the waiter, 'I'd like to send my compliments to the chef. It's the first time I've ever been served roast beef, ice cream and coffee all at the same temperature!'

Riddles

I said, 'What has four legs, howls at the moon and is full of cement?' He

Restaurants

I said, 'Does the orchestra play anything on request?' The waiter said, 'Yes, sir ... is there anything you would like them to play?' I said, 'Tell them to play dominoes until I've finished eating!'

Three fellows were sitting in a restaurant. The first one told the waiter to bring him a steak ... thick and rare. The second one said, 'I'll have one too, but make it thicker and rarer.' The third one said, 'Just bring the bull out here and I'll bite it as it goes by!'

Three guys went into a restaurant for a cup of tea. One wanted his very hot, the second wanted his very strong and the third said, 'Waiter, just be sure the cup is clean.' The waiter came back with the three cups of tea and said, 'Who asked for the clean cup?'

A man walked into a restaurant, sat down, ate all the rolls on the table and washed them down with water. The waiter came over and said, 'Would you like to order now, sir?' He said 'No, I'm just waiting for a friend.' This went on every day for several days. He came in, sat at the table, ate the rolls, drank the water and told the waiter he was waiting for a friend. On the sixth day he walked in, but there were no rolls on the table. He called the waiter over and said, 'What happened? Where are the rolls?' The waiter said, 'Your friend just left!'

I went into a restaurant to order some roast beef. The waiter said, 'Take the chicken pie instead.' I said, 'I don't like chicken pie. Give me the roast beef.' The waiter said, 'Take the chicken pie.' I said, 'But I don't want chicken pie. Let me talk to the head waiter.' The head waiter came over and said, 'What can I do for you, sir?' and I said, 'I'd like some roast beef.' And the head waiter said, 'Take the chicken pie instead.' I said, 'Damn it, I don't want chicken pie. I want roast beef. Let me talk to the manager!' So the manager came over and said, 'May I help you, sir?' and I said, 'Yes. I asked the waiter for roast beef and he insisted I take the chicken pie instead. I asked the head waiter for roast beef and he

Rain

Rain is quite wonderful. It makes the flowers grow. It also makes cabs disappear!

The good thing about rain is that you don't have to shovel it!

I never mind the rain, but I get nervous when my next door neighbour starts collecting animals two by two.

It rained so hard, people were jumping into the river to keep from drowning!

Religion

My wife is so religious we can't get any fire insurance. There are too many candles in the house.

I used to be an atheist, but I gave it up ... no holidays!

He's a very religious guy ... he worships money!

A guy asked me if I was a Jehovah's Witness. I said, 'I didn't even see the accident!'

Remarks (heard on planes)

Height never bothers me ... it's the space between me and the ground that gets me nervous!

Who cares what time we land so long as it's on wheels!

I'm not nervous ... my lip always bleeds when I bite it!

What do they mean? We'll have to lighten the load!

Can I open my eyes now?

R is for Religion

Quarrel

My wife's a magician ... she can turn anything into an argument!

I said to my wife, 'I've been thinking it over since this quarrel started and I have to say that everything you said was right.' She said, 'It's too late ... I've changed my mind!'

You can't hear an angry word from the couple next door ... their house is soundproof!

The judge said, 'What started the trouble between you and the plaintiff?' The defendant said, 'Well, it was like this, your honour. He threw a cup of hot coffee over me, I hit him in the face with my bag of tools, then he broke a chair over my head, and the next thing we knew we were quarrelling!'

Questions & Answers

What have you been doing?
This and that.
When?
Now and then.
And where have you been doing it?
Here and there!

When a woman marries a man, why does she take his name?
Why not? She takes everything else he's got!

Quiz Show

I won my wife in a quiz show. She had on a white dress. I thought she was a refrigerator!

The quizmaster said, 'What's the first thing you'll do with the money you've won?' I said, 'I'll count it!'

I read that one guy lost 64,000 pounds in a quiz ... the income tax men were doing the quizzing!

What happens when the human body is immersed in water?

The telephone rings!

Q is for Question

I told my psychiatrist that I was always having an argument with my wife and it was driving me mad. He said, 'What do you argue about?' I said, 'It's always before going to bed – the cold cream, the facial lotions, the hair curlers.' He said, 'Well, what does she say to you?' I said, 'I don't care what she says. I'm not giving up my facials and my curlers for anyone!'

When I was a kid I went to a psychiatrist for one of those aptitude tests. On the desk he put a pitchfork, a wrench and a hammer and he said to the nurse, 'If he grabs the pitchfork he'll become a farmer. If he grabs the wrench he'll be a mechanic and if he takes the hammer he'll be a carpenter.' I grabbed the nurse!

A woman went to a psychiatrist and said, 'I'm worried about my husband. He thinks he's a washing machine. He keeps rolling his head around and around, back and forth, around and around, and soap and hot water keep coming out of his ears.' He said, 'Oh, I don't think that's anything to worry about.' She said, 'But, doctor, he isn't getting the sheets clean!'

I met a psychiatrist who's a real specialist. He only treats hikers, hunters and campers. Instead of a couch he uses a sleeping bag!

O
P

A woman went to a psychiatrist and complained her husband was always putting an egg in his milk shake. He said, 'So what's wrong with that? Lots of people mix an egg with their milk shake.' She said, 'A fried egg?'

The psychiatrist told me I could consider myself cured. I said, 'Are you kidding? Before I came to you I was Napoleon. Now I'm just another nobody!'

The psychiatrist said, 'What makes you nervous?' I said, 'All day long I'm hearing voices and I don't know where they're coming from.' He said, 'How often does this happen?' I said, 'Whenever I answer the phone!'

Priest

A priest was halfway through his sermon when he saw a man asleep in the front row. He asked the fellow next to him if he would be so kind as to wake him up, but the fellow said, 'I'm sorry, father, but that wouldn't be fair.' The priest said, 'And why not?' The fellow said, 'Well, you put him to sleep ... you wake him up!'

Private Purposes

See Introduction: page 11

Producer

My producer gave me a twenty pound note and told me to get him a sandwich, get something for myself and bring him the change. I came back, gave him the sandwich and fifty pence change. He said, 'That can't be right.' I said, 'You told me to get something for myself, so I bought a shirt and tie!'

Psychiatrists

I spent ten thousand pound on psychiatrists and then found all I needed to solve my problems was ten thousand pounds in the first place!

A woman sent her husband to a psychiatrist because he kept thinking he was a cannibal. When he came back, she said, 'Well, what was he like?' He said, 'Delicious!'

Psychiatrists tell us that one out of every five people is emotionally disturbed. The reason is that the other four are nuts!

I went to my psychiatrist the other day and said, 'Can you cure me of my phobia?' He said, 'What phobia?' I said, 'I can't stand nuts.' He said, 'Neither can I ... get out!'

Plumber

The plumber asked the woman, 'Where's the drip?' She said, 'He's in the bathroom trying to fix the leak!'

Policemen

This guy walked up to me the other night and said, 'Quick! Did you see a policeman around here?' I said, 'No.' He said, 'Good! Stick 'em up!'

This fellow walked into a police station and asked to see the man who'd been arrested for breaking into his house the night before. The sergeant said, 'And why would you want to do that?' He said, 'So I can find out how he got into my house without waking my wife ... I've been trying to do that for twenty years!'

A policeman stopped a woman for speeding. She said, 'I wasn't doing ninety.' He said, 'I'm going to give you a ticket for trying!'

This officer stopped me and said, 'Why are you driving with a bucket of water on the passenger seat?' I said, 'So that I can dip my headlights!'

O
P

Portrait Painter

This woman went to a portrait painter and said, 'I want you to paint me with my face resting on my hands, showing each finger with a different kind of diamond ring, and on my wrist should be bracelets made of diamonds, rubies, emeralds and pearls, right up to the elbow.' The painter said, 'Did you bring the jewellery with you?' She said, 'Don't be silly. Who said anything about jewellery? It's just that when I die, I want my husband's next wife to go crazy trying to find out where I hid it all!'

This woman was having her portrait painted and after sitting for five hours she turned to the painter and said, 'Well, does it look like me?' He said, 'It looked like you two hours ago! Now I'm trying to improve it!'

sailor was determined to have this parrot and bid thirty. The other bidder came back with thirty-five and the sailor upped the bid to fifty. This went on and on for some time, but the sailor was determined to have the parrot and he finally won the lot. He settled up with the auctioneer and said, 'I paid a lot of money for this bird. Are you sure it can talk?' The cashier said, 'Can he talk? Who do you think was bidding against you?'

An old lady bought a parrot and all the parrot could say was, 'Who is it?' No matter what you asked the parrot, that's all he knew. 'Who is it? Who is it?' One day the plumber came to the door and knocked and the parrot yelled, 'Who is it?' He said, 'It's the plumber.' The parrot kept asking, 'Who is it? Who is it?' and the plumber kept answering back, 'It's the plumber. It's the plumber.' In the end he got so exhausted he fainted on the front porch. A crowd gathered and one of them said, 'Who is it?' The parrot yelled, 'It's the plumber!'

Parties

I was at a party with so many famous people, I was the only one there I'd never heard of!

I was at a party the other night. My wife said, 'Stop saying, "One more for the road." We live here!'

Photography

Two photographers were comparing notes at the end of the day. One said, 'I saw a very sad sight this morning. I was standing on Waterloo Bridge when an old man came up to me and asked me for money. He was trembling with cold, his clothes were threadbare and he hadn't eaten for days. My heart went out to him.' The other said, 'What did you give him?' He said, 'A thousandth of a second at focus 3 point 5!'

Palladium

I'll never forget when I was playing the Palladium ... I drew a line a mile long, but the manager made me go out and erase it!

Parking

I read the other day that only three out of ten murderers get caught. But if you park in the wrong place nine out of ten people get caught. In other words, I reckon it's safer to kill somebody!

One day the wife came home late and said she'd parked the car in Oxford Street. I said, 'Why didn't you park nearer the house?' She said, 'It was so dark over there, I couldn't find all the parts!'

I discovered a great way to avoid getting parking tickets ... remove your windscreen wiper!

The parking situation is getting so bad some guys are carrying bicycles in their cars to get to and from the parking places!

They haven't finished installing all the parking meters around town ... the truck that carries them can't find a place to park!

I bought a raffle ticket the other day. The second prize is a car. The first prize is a parking space!

Parrots

A sailor went to an auction sale where they were selling lots of pets. This magnificent parrot came under the hammer. The sailor started the bidding with ten pounds. Another bidder raised it to twenty-five, but the

P is for Policeman

Operating Theatre

A medical student was working his way through college by moonlighting in a butcher's shop. He worked in the butcher's shop by day, then changed from one white outfit into another and worked as an orderly in the hospital at night. One night he had to wheel a patient into surgery. The poor woman looked up from the trolley, saw the student and screamed, 'Help ... it's my butcher!'

Optician

I broke my glasses when I dropped them. I said to the optician, 'Will I have to be examined all over again?' He said, 'No, just your eyes!'

Onions

Do you know the difference between a lawyer and an onion? You cry when you cut up an onion!

My wife is so ugly she made an onion cry!

Opera

This singer went to Rome to study opera. When he sang his first aria in public, the audience shouted, 'Sing it again,' so he obliged. Again they yelled, 'Sing it again,' so he sang it a second time. This went on for half a dozen times until he begged to be excused. He said, 'I'm sorry, I just can't sing it again!' Then a voice in the balcony yelled out, 'You're going to sing it again until you get it right!'

I took my little boy to the opera. The conductor started to wave his baton and the big fat lady on the stage started to sing her heart out. He said, 'Dad, why is he hitting that woman with that stick?' I said, 'He isn't hitting her. He's just conducting the band.' My little boy said, 'Then what is she screaming for?'

The other night I went to the opera ... that's where, when a guy gets stabbed, he doesn't bleed, he sings!

I was in an opera once. I was in The Barber of Seville. I played a jar of Brylcreem!

One-Liners

I said, 'Don't you recognise me?' He said, 'Is there a reward?'

I've got news for you ... I just heard from Bill Bailey and he isn't coming home!

I feel like doing something wild tonight ... like taking a bath in Pepsi Cola!

He's a second-hand dealer. The first hand he lets you win, but watch out for that second hand!

I went into a country pub yesterday and ate a ploughman's lunch.
He wasn't half mad!

I'm tired ... I've been on my feet all day. It's the only way I can stand up!

I'm not myself tonight ... you probably noticed the improvement!

I'm tired – I got up the wrong side of the floor!

Where there's smoke – there's toast!

I'm so excited about my new job, I won't be able to sleep all day!

Time is relative. I know – I've got a relative doing time!

I served 87 cups of tea – I must get a new tea bag!

He offered me a job right up my alley, but who wants to work up an alley?

It was so foggy in Scotland, this fellow milked three cows before he found out he wasn't playing the bagpipes!

O is for One - Liner

Jack was nimble,
Jack was quick,
Jack jumped out of the window quick ...
... her husband came home!

Thirty days have September,
April, June and November.
All the rest have thirty-one
...except Jane Russell, who has a perfect 36!

Rock-a-bye, baby,
On the tree top,
When the bough breaks ...
... you'll shout 'Timber!' if you've got any sense!

Roses are red,
Violets are blue,
Orchids cost three-fifty,
Won't daisies do?

M
N

Jack and Jill
Went up the hill.
The last I heard
They were up there still!

Old King Cole was a merry old soul
And a merry old soul was he.
He called for his pipe
And he called for his bowl
And he called and he called and he called ... !

Humpty Dumpty sat on a wall,
Humpty Dumpty had a great fall;
All the King's horses
And all the King's men ...
... had scrambled eggs!

Nursery Rhymes

There was an old woman
Who lived in a shoe,
She had so many children
Her baby sitters' bill came to goodness knows how many pounds!

Little Miss Muffet
Sat on a tuffet,
Eating her curds and whey;
Along came a spider,
Who sat down beside her ...
... 'Is this seat taken?'

Little Miss Muffet
Sat on a tuffet,
Around her was fog and mist;
Along came a spider,
Who sat down beside her
And offered to teach her the Twist!

Mary had a little lamb ...
... boy, was she surprised ... she was expecting a baby!

Mary, Mary, quite contrary,
How does your garden grow?
... 'None of your damn business!'

Little Jack Horner
Sat in a corner
Eating his Christmas pie.
He put in his thumb
And pulled out a plum
And said, 'But I ordered apple!'

Neighbours

The only time we see our neighbours is when we try to borrow back our lawnmower!

Night

A hunter woke up a farmer in the middle of the night and yelled, 'I'm sorry to wake you, but it's very cold and I'd like to stay here for the night.' The farmer slammed down the window and said, 'Well, stay there!'

Nudist

This fellow went up to a nudist colony and said, 'I want to join.' The guy on the gate said, 'You can't join with that blue suit on.' He said, 'What blue suit? I'm cold!'

Numbers

Seven's my lucky number. I was born on the 7th day of the 7th month in the year 1917. Last night I dreamed I kissed 7 girls, so today I bet on the 7th horse in the 7th race. The horse was called 'Seventh Heaven.' It came in seventh!

I'm a member of the Secret Six. It's so secret, I don't even know the other five!

Nurse

When I had a cold I rang the doctor and the nurse answered. I said, 'I think I have a temperature.' She said, 'Take off all your clothes and get into bed!' *But she never showed up!*

N is for Night

I used to be a one man band. I played the drums with my feet, the harmonica with my mouth, the tambourine with my elbows and the vibraphone with my knees. What did I do with my hands? I held them to my ears!

Some people can make a piano talk, but I can make a piano laugh ... I tickle the ivories!

I can tell the time from my piano. Every morning when I start to play someone bangs on the wall and yells, 'Hey, stop making that noise at two o'clock in the morning!'

I bought a piano stool the other day ... I can't get a single note out of it!

When I play the accordion I always cry ... it keeps pinching my stomach!

He plays the hottest trumpet in town ... he stole it only last week!

My uncle was a great conductor ... he was struck by lightning!

He's a relief piano player ... it's a relief when he stops!

When I was in New York, a fellow walked up to me and said, 'Excuse me, but how do you get to Carnegie Hall?' I said, 'Practice!'

I took saxophone lessons for six months until I dislocated my jaw. How did I know I was supposed to blow in the small end?

A piano tuner was called to a nightclub to tune the piano. He was at it for five hours, but the bill only came to three pounds. The manager said 'Is that all? How come you worked for five hours to tune the piano and you only charge three pounds?' He said, 'What?'

I made a killing in the stock market ... I shot my broker!

The mechanic gave me an estimate of one hundred pounds to fix my car. The next day he gave me a bill for two hundred. I said, 'How about the estimate you gave me yesterday for one hundred?' He said, 'Oh yes, I forgot! That makes it three hundred!'

Money isn't everything. I've got something money can't buy ... poverty!

Motorcycle

The trouble with my wife is that she's a terrible backseat driver ... so I decided to buy a motorbike and sidecar. But this didn't stop her going yackety-yak all the time. Yackety-yak! Yackety-yak! One day a policeman pulled me over and said, 'Hey, your wife fell out of the sidecar six miles back.' I said, 'Thank God! I thought I was going deaf!'

Music and Musicians

He's one of the best arrangers in the business. He arranges all the chairs for the band!

He used to have a three piece combo ... an organ, a cup and a monkey!

I asked the pianist if he played by ear. He said, 'No, my neck isn't long enough!'

Now I'm going to play like I've never played before ... because I've never played before!

For years I used to run up and down the scales with my fingers. I used to work in a fish shop!

Memory

My memory's terrible. I have to look at the mail before I can remember my own name!

Every comedian comes out and says, 'A funny thing happened to me on the way to the theatre this evening.' Well, a funny thing happened to me on the way to the theatre this evening ... I forgot my act!

My wife has a terrible memory. She never forgets a single thing she tells me to do!

I've got a terrible memory. I cut myself shaving today and I forgot to bleed!

Men

He never smiles. Not because he has bad teeth ... it's just that his gums don't fit!

He has a speech impediment ... every time he opens his mouth his wife interrupts!

He may talk like an idiot and look like an idiot, but don't let it fool you ... he is an idiot!

I know a guy who shaves thirty times a day ... he's a barber!

Money

I know a guy whose wife made him a millionaire ... before that he was a multi-millionaire!

Marriage

They've been married for twenty years and they still feel the same – they can't stand each other!

This woman was dying. She called her husband to her bed and said, 'Sam, I've been unfaithful to you.' He said, 'So? What do you think I gave you poison for?'

There were ten chorus girls. Nine of them married millionaires. They got diamonds, furs, expensive holidays. Only one of them married a poor man. And, would you believe it, she's the only one who's miserable!

This guy bought his wife a burial plot for her birthday. The following year when he bought her nothing, she complained. He said, 'What are you complaining about? You didn't use the present I bought you last year!'

This woman went on holiday leaving her husband behind. Before she left she told him to take special care of her pet Siamese cat. As soon as she arrived she phoned home to ask after the cat. Her husband said, 'The cat just died!' She burst into tears and started to read the riot act to him: 'How can you be so blunt? Why couldn't you have broken the news gradually? Today you could have said it was playing on the roof. Tomorrow you could have added that it fell off the roof and broke a leg. Then on the third day you could have said the poor thing had passed away in the night. You could have been more sensitive about the whole thing. By the way, how's my mother?' He said, 'She's playing on the roof!'

We've been married for 20 years and she still wears a ponytail. She's certainly got the face for it!

M is for Marriage

Letters

Dear Agony Aunt, Ten years ago I sent my husband out for a loaf of bread and he hasn't come back since. What shall I do? ... *Don't wait any longer. Send out for another loaf of bread!*

Liar

This guy said, 'If a fellow called you a liar, what would you do?' I said, 'What size fellow?'

Library

K
L

Society people usually have dinner at eight and then coffee is served in the library. I always thought the library closed at seven!

I said to the librarian, 'Have you got a book on butterflies?' She said, 'Yes.' I said, 'Well, take it off ... you'll crush them to death!'

Love Bites

See Introduction: page 12

Luck

I'm so unlucky ... one day
I called the speaking clock and
the recording hung up on me!

I'm the sort of fellow who gets
paper-cuts from get well cards!

The jury returned to the courtroom after being out for three days. The judge said, 'Have you reached a decision?' The foreman said, 'Yes, your honour. We've decided not to become involved.'

He said, 'I'm a lawyer of twenty years standing.' I said, 'You must be tired ... sit down!'

The lawyer asked the prisoner what his trade was. He said, 'I'm a locksmith.' Then the lawyer asked him what he was doing inside the premises when the police raided them. He said, 'I was making a bolt for the door!'

The first lawyer said, 'As soon as I realised it was a crooked business, I got out of it.' The second lawyer said, 'How much?'

The judge said to the pickpocket, 'How is it you took that man's watch from his pocket without him knowing it?' He said, 'I can't give out that information, your honour. My fee is one hundred pounds for the full course of ten lessons!'

Laziness

I'm not afraid of hard work. I could fall asleep right beside it!

This guy said, 'Are you in favour of a five day week?' I said, 'No. I'm in favour of a five day weekend!'

The fellow next door said, 'What was that terrible noise I heard at your house last night?' I said, 'That was my wife washing my clothes.' He said, 'Why should that cause so much noise?' I said, 'I was too lazy to get out of them!'

I missed my nap today. I slept right through it!

Languages

I learned Japanese with records that play while you sleep. It works. Now I speak perfect Japanese, but only when I'm asleep!

This rich old lady sent her pet poodle to a language school to learn a foreign language. Her friend said, 'This is ridiculous. How can a poor dumb animal learn a foreign language?' and the poodle looked up and said, 'Meow!'

Laundry

I feel like a changed man ... I just got my laundry back!

I was really surprised when my laundry sent back a dozen shirts without a single button missing. I only sent them a pair of shorts!

I always get my laundry back the same day. They keep refusing it!

Jack the Ripper never died ... he's doing my shirts!

Law

A man was brought into court for disturbing the peace. The judge said, 'What I would like to know is what induced you to climb to the top of a flagpole, play the saxophone, shout at the people walking by and disturb everyone by singing at the top of your voice.' He said, 'Well, it's like this, your honour. If I didn't do something like this once in a while, I'd go crazy!'

The judge asked the defendant why he hit his wife with a heavy lamp. He said, 'Because the piano was too heavy!'

L is for Law

K
L

Knowledge

Did you know that a female herring lays about 35,000 eggs at one time? If those herrings were a little bit smarter, they could take over the world!

People learn something new every day ... why just today my wife learned that a car won't climb a telephone pole!

I'm studying anthropology. I went into our local library and said, 'Do you keep books on pygmies?' The girl said, 'No, only on shelves!'

Space is where there is nothing. I can't exactly explain it to you, but I've got it right here in my head!

Kissing

She said, 'How come when
I kiss you your lips burn
like fire?' I said, 'Well, maybe
I ought to take the cigarette
out of my mouth!'

I asked her how she learned
to kiss like that. She said she
used to blow up footballs!

She said, 'Who told you that
you could kiss me?' I said,
'Just about everybody!'

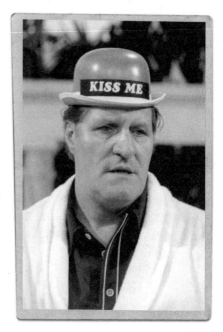

Kleptomania

A kleptomaniac was treated by a psychiatrist and after a while he was
discharged as cured. He said, 'I'd like to do something for you to show
my gratitude.' The doctor said, 'Well, I really don't want anything, but if
you ever get a relapse, I could use a transistor radio!'

Knight

In days of old when knights were bold ... the king turned to his knight
and said, 'What have you been doing today?' The knight said, 'I have
been robbing and pillaging on your behalf, burning the villages of your
enemies in the north.' The king said, 'But I don't have any enemies in
the north.' The knight said, 'I'm afraid you do now!'

Kangaroos

He said, 'What does a kangaroo eat for breakfast?' I said, 'I don't know.'
He said, 'Pouched eggs!'

A mother kangaroo turned to her friend and said, 'I hate it when it's raining and the kids have to play inside!'

A kangaroo kept escaping from his enclosure at the zoo. The keepers put up this fence that was ten feet high, but the kangaroo still escaped. The next day they put up a twenty-foot fence, and he still got free. The monkey in the next enclosure said, 'How high do you think they'll go?' The kangaroo said, 'It doesn't matter until someone remembers to lock the gate at night!'

He said, 'Why was the mother kangaroo cross with her children?' I said, 'I don't know.' He said, 'Because they ate biscuits in bed!'

Karate

I always say that if you practise breaking boards in half with your bare hand, you'll be able to look after yourself when a board attacks you!

I know a priest who took up karate. He became so good at it, when he went to bless himself he broke his nose!

My wife is so good at karate, last week she stuck her hand out to make a left turn and cut a truck in half!

Then there was the karate expert who joined the army. When he gave his first salute, he killed himself!

When I first met my wife, I got a lump in my throat ... she was a karate expert!

K is for Karate

Jungley!!

A big lion was roaring through the jungle one day with this chip on his shoulder. Every animal he came across, he'd stop them and say, 'Who is the King of the Jungle?' and he was told that he was. Finally he bumped into a mean, nasty-tempered elephant. So he stopped him and said, 'Hey, Jumbo, who is the King of the Jungle?' So the elephant grabbed the lion with his trunk, tossed him into the air half a dozen times and then slammed him against a big tree. The lion picked himself up and said, 'Look, there's no good getting sore about it, just because you don't know the answer!'

A hunter came across a lion in the jungle and began to pray. Then the lion started to pray too. He turned to the hunter and said, 'Don't get me wrong ... I always say grace before meals!'

Two guys – Tom and Harry – went lion hunting in Africa and one night Harry bet Tom a fiver that he'd be the first one to go out and kill a lion. They made the bet and Harry went out with his rifle. After about an hour, a lion poked his head into the tent and said, 'Hey, do you know a guy named Harry?' Tom said, 'Yes, I do. Why?' and the lion said, 'Well, he owes you a fiver!'

Two guys were hunting for lions in Africa and got themselves a hut right on the edge of the jungle. After a short while one of them was seen tearing back to the hut with a big roaring lion running after him. The hunter fell through the open door and the lion shot past him into the hut. Quick as a flash, the hunter got up, rushed outside and slammed the door behind him. As he ran off, he yelled back to his friend inside, 'You skin that one, while I go after another one!'

This chap was out of work. He couldn't get a job anywhere. Then one day he was walking along the road and he passed this building site. He went up to this fellow who was working there and said, 'Excuse me, I was wondering if you were looking for any men for this job.' The fellow said, 'Well, as it happens, they are looking for labourers. Why don't you see the foreman over there? He'll fix you up. But there's just one thing. It's a company rule. They'll only take you on if you know someone who's already working on the site. Otherwise you're wasting your time.' So he walked across to the foreman and said, 'Excuse me. I was wondering if there were any jobs going.' The foreman said, 'As a matter of fact there are. When can you start?' He said, 'Straightaway.' The foreman said, 'Right! By the way there's just one thing. We only take on people who know someone already working on the site. Is there anyone here you recognise?' The chap didn't know a soul, but he suddenly heard this Irish guy working nearby. He said, 'I know him!' The foreman said, 'What's his name then?' He said, 'His name is Dare.' The foreman said, 'Well, give him a call.' The chap said, 'Alright.' So he gave the Irishman a wave and shouted, 'Hallo, Dare.' The Irishman replied, 'Hallo dare yourself!' and the chap got the job!

I know a guy who has the hardest job in the world. He sells Venetian blinds for submarines.

I got a job once selling doorbells door to door. Unfortunately when I rang, the people who needed what I had to sell didn't know I was there!

Jokes on Jokes

You know what you have to go through to be a comedian? A lot of old joke books!

My wife knows my jokes backwards ... and that's how she tells them!

Jester

What do you call an out-of-work jester? Nobody's fool!

Jewellery

A shoplifter was caught stealing a watch. He begged the jeweller not to call the police and said he would happily pay for it. He was taken to the cashier and given a bill. He took one look and said, 'Goodness, that's a little more than I can afford. Can't you show me something a little cheaper?'

Jobs

I said to my boss, 'My wife and I find it very hard for two people to live on my salary.' He got us a divorce!

The boss asked me how much I wanted, so I quoted him a price in six figures. He picked one and we made a deal!

He used to be a night-watchman, but he got fired. Someone stole two nights!

He says he has hundreds of people under him ... he's a watchman in a cemetery!

It must be wonderful to be an undertaker. Where else can you go to work and find everything laid out for you?

There was this fellow. One day his wife said, 'Get out of bed and get a job.' His friend said, 'So what happened? Did you go out and get a job?' He said, 'Are you kidding? Where can you find a job at five o'clock in the afternoon?'

J is for Jester

He has been in films, he has been on radio, he has been on television ... he's probably the biggest has-been in the business!

There's no end to his talent ... and no beginning either!

Inventions

I've just invented a chemical that is so powerful it destroys anything it touches ... but I can't find anything to keep it in!

I've just invented a new noiseless alarm clock. It doesn't ring. It has a big eye that stares at you till you wake up!

I've just invented a pen with a meatball point. It writes under gravy!

I've just invented a stepladder without steps for cleaning windows on the ground floor!

My father invented a burglar alarm, but someone stole it!

The thermos flask is a great invention. How does it know when to keep things hot and when to keep them cold?

Electricity is a wonderful thing. Do you realise that if we didn't have electricity, we'd be watching television by candlelight?

I see they've invented a new cigarette. The whole thing is a filter ... only the tip contains tobacco!

I've just invented plastic song sheets ... for people who like to sing in the shower!

I said, 'I've just taken out a £10,000 policy.' He said, 'Accident?'
I said, 'No – on purpose!'

I have a policy that states that if I bang my head, they pay me a lump sum!

Interior Decorator

This woman went to an interior decorator and had great trouble getting
what she wanted. She finally opened up and confessed that her husband
thought he was a bear. The decorator said, 'A bear? Why don't you go
to a psychiatrist?' She said, 'Do you think he can tell me what colour
scheme will work in a cave?'

Introductions

She plays the piano by ear ... but sometimes her earrings get in the way!

Our next act needs no introduction, because he hasn't shown up!

Our next act comes to us direct from America where he was hailed by
thousands of people. He was driving a taxi!

Five producers wanted our next act to go to Hollywood and make a picture,
but they found out she couldn't paint!

After playing the accordion all his life, our next act took up the piano.
Every time he hung it round his neck, it nearly killed him!

It gives me great pleasure to introduce our next act. We will now have
a one minute intermission to give you all a chance to say, 'Who cares?'

I was awake half the night trying to remember something I wanted to do. Then about five o'clock in the morning it suddenly dawned on me ... I had planned to go to bed early!

Insults

As for my agent, I've seen poultry better dressed than he is!

He's so tightfisted, he's got varicose veins in his knuckles!

Insurance

I
J

I've got the only policy that pays me a thousand pounds if I get hit by a satellite while singing 'How High the Moon'!

I'm covered with insurance policies up to here. One day I'll cover the rest of me!

I cancelled my Fire Insurance Policy because they wouldn't pay a claim. I claimed that all the cigars I smoked last year were destroyed by fire!

Burglars broke into our house and I was told I couldn't collect a penny. The agent said I had Fire and Theft policies, when I should have had Fire or Theft. That means the only way I'd collect would be if we were robbed while the house was burning down!

Insurance policies are great. You pay and you pay and when you die you have nothing to worry about for the rest of your life!

An insurance salesman wants to sell me a retirement policy. If I keep up the payments for ten years, he'll be able to retire!

Insomnia

My insomnia is getting so bad, I can't even sleep when it's time to get up!

I'm cured now, but I lie awake half the night thinking of how I used to suffer from it!

If you've got insomnia, don't lose any sleep over it!

They've got a new cure for insomnia ... a pill that weighs two hundred pounds. You don't swallow it. You drop it on your head!

I couldn't sleep a wink last night. I took a sleeping pill and I dreamt all night that I was awake!

Ignition

Two drunks were sitting at a bar when one said to the other, 'Does your tongue burn?' The other said, 'I don't know. I've never been drunk enough to light it!'

Indians

The Lone Ranger and Tonto rode into a spot of bother. On all sides they were surrounded by hostile Indians. The Lone Ranger said, 'Well, kemosabe, it looks like the end of the trail. Those Indians are about to close in. We've had it.' Tonto said, 'You mean you've had it, white man!'

An Indian chief walked into a restaurant. The waiter said, 'Do you have a reservation?' He said, 'Certainly ... in Arizona!'

There was an Indian chief called Running Water. He had two sons named Hot and Cold and a nephew, Lukewarm!

An Indian chief had two sons, Straight Arrow and Falling Rocks. The day came when he told them to go out into the world and make a name for themselves. In time Straight Arrow came back, but Falling Rocks never returned. They're still looking for him. That's why everywhere you go in the Wild West you see signs saying, 'Watch out for Falling Rocks'!

Insects

I feel like a mosquito in a nudist colony ... I don't know where to begin!

Two fleas were going shopping. One said, 'Shall we walk or take a dog?'

I is for Indian

I went into my room and rang straightaway for the manager. I said, 'Does the water always come through the roof like that?' He said, 'Only when it rains!'

This hotel was so big, by the time I got to my room I owed two days rent!

I said to the receptionist, 'I want a full-length mirror put in my room right away.' She said, 'But you've already got a half-length mirror. What's wrong with that?' I said, 'Three times this week I've gone out without my trousers on!'

G
H

My room was so small I couldn't brush my teeth sideways!

Hypochondria

A hypochondriac went to see his doctor. The doctor said, 'Well, what do you think is the matter with you today?' He said, 'I don't know ... what's new?'

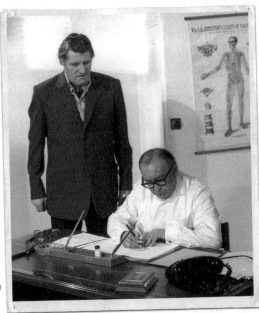

I knew a hypochondriac who wouldn't visit the Dead Sea until he found out what it died of!

He's such a hypochondriac, he has a vaccination before he goes to a foreign movie!

Hospitals

I saw a sign in a hospital the other day that read, 'Visitors only from two to five.' Isn't that silly? Who wants visitors that young?

Hotels

I've stayed at every hotel in the country and I've got the towels to prove it!

The hotel was fine, but the towels were so thick, you couldn't close your suitcase!

I stayed at a hotel and they gave me a room facing north ... it had no roof!

I couldn't sleep ... too many people kept coming in all night to wash their hands!

I said, 'Is this room service?' The girl said, 'Yes.' I said, 'Send up a room.'

There was a sign in the room: 'Don't slam the door ... it's holding up the walls!'

It was really warm in my room. I tried to open the window, but it was stuck. It wouldn't budge. So I finally took an aspirin to ease the pane!

I said to the porter, 'What's the idea of giving me one black shoe and one brown shoe?' He said, 'I'm sorry, sir. That's the second time that's happened this morning!'

I said to the receptionist, 'Is the room rate really ten pounds a day?' She said, 'No, it's ten pounds for the night ... we throw the day in for free.'

G
H

I bet on a horse that was so slow. The jockey kept hitting it with his whip and the horse said, 'What are you doing that for? There's nobody behind us!'

A man paid £5,000 for a racehorse and entered it in a £10,000 race. The horse came last. So he entered it in a £5,000 race and it came last again. So he entered it in a £1,000 race and it came last once more. He went to the horse and said, 'Look, I'm going to enter you in a £500 race and if you lose this one, tomorrow morning you'll be pulling a milk cart.' The race began and the horse was so far behind that the jockey began to hit him with the whip. The horse looked back and said, 'Hey, take it easy ... I've got to be up at five o'clock!'

Home

I live in one of those reversible penthouses. It's in the basement!

My agent ... his home is so big, when it's five o'clock in the kitchen, it's six o'clock in the living room!

Honesty

Honesty is the best policy. The only time I ever found anything ... it was a wallet with a hundred pounds. So I put an ad in the 'lost and found' column of a newspaper ... the Budapest Times!

I wouldn't believe him if he swore he was lying!

Horses

You know what a racehorse is ... an animal that can take several thousand people for a ride at the same time!

I bought a racehorse about a month ago. A friend of mine said, 'What are you going to do with it?' I said, 'I'm going to race it.' He said, 'By the look of it, I think you'll beat it!'

This fellow bet two thousand pounds on a horse and lost. I said, 'How do you feel?' He said, 'Not too grand!'

I used to have a riding school, but business kept falling off!

She said, 'Your wife won't talk to me since I took her horseback riding.' I said, 'She could be sore about something.'

I was born in the saddle ... and it wasn't easy!

Heckler-Squelchers

Some people might think you're loud and foolish ... and I agree with them!

There's a rumour going around that he had a mother!

He's good to his mother ... he brings home everything he steals!

Did you ever get the feeling that the world was a tuxedo and you were a pair of brown shoes?

I live down by the river. If you're in the neighbourhood, drop in!

(to a drunk) It's great to see a guy who can hold his lemonade like a man!

I'd put you in your place, if only I had the time and a shovel!

Was the ground cold when you came out of it this morning?

It's lucky for you I'm a gentleman ... and a coward!

Hobbies

I've got a special hobby. You know how some people collect stamps and some people collect paintings? Well, I collect dust!

Hollywood

Fred Allen once said, 'You could take all the sincerity in Hollywood and conceal it in a flea's navel and still have enough room left for six caraway seeds and an agent's heart.'

G
H

Health

He suffers from an occupational disease. Work makes him sick!

I'm recovering from a cold. I'm so full of penicillin that if I sneeze, I'll cure someone.

Every morning I like a cold bath ... filled with hot water!

I found a good cure for amnesia, but I can't remember what it is!

The best way to avoid a cold is to drink a lot of water. You never saw a fish with a cold!

All his life he had trouble with his back ... he couldn't get it off the bed!

I'm so anaemic. The other day a guy hit me on the nose. I said, 'I owe you a nose bleed!'

Heaven

This fellow died and went to heaven. When he got there, St Peter told him that before he'd be allowed in, he'd have to take a test. First, he'd have to fly twenty yards with the wings they gave him, then play three choruses of his favourite hymn on a harp, and finally walk a hundred paces with a halo on his head without it slipping. Well, he passed the flying without any trouble and played not three, but six choruses of the hymn on the harp, but he just couldn't get the halo to stay straight when he walked. St Peter said, 'I'm sorry, we can't accept you.' The fellow said, 'Why?' St Peter said, 'Well, you're very good, but before you come in you have to get your "O" level!'

Hair

Being bald has its advantages ... you're the first one to know when it starts raining!

I used to part my hair from ear to ear. It was okay, but people kept whispering in my nose!

Halloween

On Halloween I really know how to scare people. I ring their bell and do my act!

Hats

Somebody gave me a ten gallon hat. I didn't know whether to wear it or move into it!

My wife said, 'Do you like this turned down hat?' I said, 'How much does it cost?' She said, 'Fifty pounds.' I said, 'Turn it down!'

There's nothing that goes to my wife's head faster than a new hat!

She said, 'Your hat is on the wrong way.' I said, 'How do you know which way I'm going?'

I said to the girl in the shop, 'I want to buy a hat.' She said, 'Fedora?' I said, 'No, for myself!'

She wore a hat with so many flowers on it, three funerals followed her home!

They're making a new kind of woman's hat with a live pigeon on top. If you don't pay the bill, the hat flies back to the shop!

H is for Hats

The other day I got caught in a bunker and couldn't get out. The more I tried to hit the ball, the deeper I got into the bunker. The caddy said, 'What are you doing? Digging for **diamonds**?' I said, 'Have a **heart**!' He said, 'Do you want a **club**?' I said, 'No, a **spade**!'

When I first took up golf I dug up so many worms I decided to go fishing!

I once had a caddy who kept laughing at all my strokes. I would have knocked his head off, but I didn't know which club to use!

I saw a sign on a Scottish golf course once. It said, 'Members will please refrain from picking up lost balls until after they have stopped rolling!'

I said to the caddy, 'Do you think I can get home with a 4 iron?' He said, 'I don't know ... where do you live?'

The Scotsman said to the caddy, 'How are you at finding lost balls?' He said, 'Very good, sir!' The Scotsman said, 'Well, look around and find one and we'll start the game!'

When you're swinging a golf club, there are three rules always to remember – one, keep your head down; two, keep your damn head down; and three, keep your goddamn head down.

I found out why you have to address the ball ... so that if you lose it, they'll mail it to you!

As Jack Benny once said, give me my golf clubs, the fresh air and a beautiful partner and you can keep my golf clubs and the fresh air!

I went into a shop and bought a golf ball. The man said, 'Shall I wrap it?' I said, 'No, I'll drive it home!'

One day I was spraying my lawn and my neighbour asked me what I was using. I said, 'It's a secret formula to keep away elephants.' He said, 'But we don't get elephants around here.' I said, 'See how effective it is!'

There's nothing I like more on a warm summer's day than to put on my old clothes and a big shady hat, get out all the tools, settle down in a deckchair with a long cool drink and then tell the gardener where to dig!

Ghosts

These two ghosts used to walk around together with their heads under their arms. One day they slept late, got up in a hurry and grabbed the wrong heads. Later that night, one of them said, 'Here, guess what I've done?' The other said, 'I already know. I'm ahead of you!'

Giraffe

Do you know what's worse than a giraffe with a sore throat? A centipede with fallen arches!

Girls

I took her to Paris to see the Venus de Milo. She said, 'I'd like to look like her.' So I broke both her arms!

She's a cover girl ... the more her face is covered, the better she looks!

Golf

I played a little golf this morning. First I teed off and I made a hole in one. Then I teed off again and I made another hole. Then I covered up both holes and went home!

Gambling

In Las Vegas they gamble everywhere. I went into a drug store for an aspirin and the girl behind the counter said, 'I'll toss you, double or nothing.' I lost. I came out with two headaches!

When I was in Las Vegas I was so unlucky I even lost money in the stamp machine!

Gambling has brought our family closer together. We had to move to a smaller house!

He's a second-hand dealer. The first hand he lets you win. But watch out for that second hand!

This fellow went into a betting shop and put one hundred pounds on a horse at twenty to one ... and he won two thousand pounds. He collected his winnings, came out of the shop and bumped into an old tramp. He said, 'Oh, I'm sorry. I've just won two thousand pounds on a horse and I was so excited I didn't see you.' The tramp said, 'Two thousand pounds?' He said, 'Yes, would you like to hold it for a moment?' The tramp said, 'I'd love to ... just to feel it in my hands for a moment ... two thousand pounds!' As he moved forward to take the money, the tramp suddenly turned white and fainted. A woman passed by and said, 'What's wrong with him?' The guy said, 'I don't know. He didn't feel two grand!'

Gardening

I took up gardening and all I grew was tired!

I love the sound of a lawnmower. It means that something is being done and I'm not doing it!

G is for Giraffe

Fortune Tellers

She told me she reads tea leaves. I didn't even know you could write on them!

I went to a fortune teller and she looked at my hands. She said, 'Your future looks pretty black!' I said, 'Are you kidding? I've still got my gloves on!'

E
F

Friends

He's the kind of friend you can always depend on ... always around when he needs you!

I just arrived from America by plane ... it's the only way to fly!

When I complained my ears hurt, the air hostess gave me some chewing gum. I'm still trying to get it out of my ears!

I was relaxing in the plane watching the clouds go by when a parachutist appeared in the aisle. He said, 'Are you going to join me?' I said, 'Thank you very much, but I'm happy where I am.' The parachutist said, 'Just as you like ... I'm the pilot!'

I always sit in the back of a plane. It's much safer. You never hear of a plane backing into a mountain!

Food

Did you ever try to eat with chopsticks? I tried it once. I didn't eat anything, but I started three fires!

The most important thing in life is food. If you ever stop to think about it, without food you can't eat!

Films

You've heard of Hopalong Cassidy ... I want you to meet Dragalong Cooper!

I had a part in 'The Big Sleep' ... I was the mattress!

The movie had a happy ending ... everybody was glad when it was over!

When I was a kid it was much easier to tell right from wrong. The good guys always rode white horses and the bad guys always rode black horses. Then some wise guy came along riding a black and white horse and I've been confused ever since!

Fire

Two businessmen were having a drink. One said, 'I'm sorry to hear about the fire that burned down your factory.' He said, 'Hold your tongue! It's not until tomorrow!'

Fishing

This guy was fishing over a flower bed. I went up and said, 'How many have you caught today?' He said, 'You're the ninth!'

I went fishing the other day and didn't catch a thing. This fellow came up and said, 'Any luck?' I said, 'I could do with a bite!' So he bit me!

Flying

I just flew in ... I should have waited for the plane!

I never go by plane ... I get dizzy just from licking an airmail stamp!

Flying doesn't scare me ... it petrifies me!

Family

Every morning my mother would get up at seven, eat her breakfast and then go to work. Then my brother Tom would get up, make his breakfast and then he'd go to work. At half past eight my brother Charlie got up, made his breakfast and he'd go to work. Then at nine o'clock my father got up, made his breakfast and he went to work. By that time I had the bed all to myself!

Last week my grandfather celebrated his 103rd birthday. Unfortunately he couldn't be there ... he died when he was thirty-nine!

My grandfather passed away when he was 103. No one expected it. His father was broken up about it!

I hate making decisions. I have an eleven-year-old daughter I haven't named yet!

Family Planning

See Introduction: page 12

Farming

It was so hot on the farm, I milked a cow and got three pints of steam!

Females

She was a gorgeous creature
And he was a doting male.
He admired her figure in English,
But he wanted to prove it in Braille!

Facts of Life

My little boy asked me how you can tell a boy fish from a girl fish. I said, 'It's all in the worms you use to catch them with. If you bait your hook with a male worm, you catch a female fish and if you use a female worm, you catch a male fish.' He said, 'But how can you tell the difference between a male worm and a female worm?' I said, 'How should I know? I only know about fish!'

When my wife was pregnant we went to see a baby doctor, but he didn't know anything. He was only eight months old!

Every time I start to explain to my little boy about the birds and the bees, he keeps switching the conversation back to girls!

Fairy Stories

A beautiful princess was walking through the woods one day when she came to a pond and heard a tiny frog speak to her. He said, 'Please take me home with you and let me sleep in your bed.' So she picked it up, carried it home and that night she placed it on her pillow. The next morning she had warts!

This fellow had fairies at the bottom of his garden. There were six of them! He used to go down there and count them every night. One night he went down there and he counted, 'One – two – three – four – five ... ' He was a fairy light!

F is for Fire

Etiquette

He said, 'Why don't you put your hand over your mouth when you yawn?' I said, 'What ... and get bitten?'

I said, 'Why were you so embarrassed when I dropped that knife in the restaurant? Lots of people drop knives.' He said, 'Not out of their sleeves!'

People ask me what is the difference between politeness and tact. Well, yesterday I walked into the wrong hotel room by mistake. A lady was taking a bath just as I opened the door. I said, 'Excuse me, sir, just like that.' Now, when I said, 'Excuse me,' that was politeness, but when I said, 'Sir,' that was tact!

My wife said, 'When the guests arrive tonight, what should I say – "Dinner is ready" or "Dinner is served"?' I said, 'If you cook like you usually do, "Dinner is ruined!"'

Exercise

I'm in tip-top shape ... but who wants to be shaped like a top?

The doctor said you need a lot of exercise, so I bought myself some golf clubs and my wife a lawnmower!

The doctor asked me what I did to keep fit. I said, 'Every morning I get up at five, I run for five miles, I exercise my arms and shoulders while I'm running, then I come back and go to the gym. I work out for half an hour, then take a cold shower and no matter how hungry I get, I don't eat a thing.' He said, 'How long have you been doing this?' I said, 'I start tomorrow!'

I said to my little boy, 'When I was your age, I thought nothing of walking five miles every day before breakfast.' Well, I don't think much of it now either!

always had my nose stuck in a book ... I couldn't afford a bookmark!

All I ever wanted out of school was myself!

Elephants

Elephants are remarkable animals. They travel for miles and miles up mountains, through jungles, and across deserts to get to the place where they're going to die and they die there! The trip kills them!

He said, 'How do you make an elephant fly?' I said, 'Well, first find a zip that's three feet long!'

My uncle used to work in the circus. He used to tell me, 'Every morning I'd get up early and carry the elephants to the water.' I said, 'Don't you mean you carried the water to the elephants?' He said, 'No wonder I was tired!'

Two drunks were in a bar. One of them was boasting what a great elephant hunter he was. He said, 'You see, elephants don't like guns. You've got to use psychology and you need four things ... a pair of binoculars, a pair of tweezers, a bucket of water and a bottle of Scotch. Then you find a nice comfortable tree and you put the bucket of water under the tree, climb up onto a big branch and sit there and wait. While you're waiting, you take a drink of Scotch. Pretty soon a big herd of elephants comes along and one elephant always stops to see what's in the bucket at the foot of the tree.' The other drunk said, 'And then what happens?' He said, 'Well, you take another drink of Scotch and then you take the binoculars and turn them around so you're looking through the wrong end. When you see the tiny little elephant at the foot of the tree, you reach down and pick him up with the tweezers. You drop him in the water and he drowns to death!'

Easter

He said, 'What did you give up for Lent?' I said, 'Fifty po[unds for the]
wife's new Easter bonnet!'

Education

Everybody took an interest in my education. My father wanted me to go
to Oxford, my mother wanted me to go to Cambridge and the truant officer
wanted me to go to school!

I can't write in the daytime ... I went to night school!

I became a man of letters ... every day I eat alphabet soup!

At the end of the day I asked the teacher, 'What did I learn today?' She
said, 'That's an odd question.' I said, 'Yes, but they'll ask me when I get
home.'

Whenever the teacher asked a question I was always the first one to raise
my hand ... unfortunately, by the time I got back to the room, someone
had already answered the question!

My father said to my mother, 'Do you think he gets his intelligence from
me?' She said, 'He must do ... I've still got mine!'

I was a genius at school. I had so many original ideas ... especially when
it came to spelling!

I always fell asleep when I went to school. My teacher used to say, 'You
can't fall asleep in my class.' I said, 'I could, if you didn't talk so loud!'

School days are the happiest days of your life ... provided your kids are
old enough to go!

E is for Education

How do I look to you? I'm just getting over a severe case of whiskey!

I know my capacity for drinking. The trouble is I get drunk before I reach it!

Why do people call Dean Martin a lush? Just because he has bourbon and cornflakes for breakfast?

I had a very bad accident. I slipped on a piece of ice. I'll never know how I got my foot in the glass!

A guy walked into a bar, ordered a double whiskey, drank it, threw a ten pound note on the table and walked out without saying a word. The barman put the note in his pocket, turned to the owner and said, 'How do you like that? He comes in here, downs a double Scotch, leaves a ten pound tip and then leaves without paying!'

Driving

Watch out for children on the roads ... they're terrible drivers!

I got hit by a hit-and-run driver. The cop said, 'Did you get his number?' I said, 'No, but I'd recognise his laugh anywhere!'

A drunk was driving his car the wrong way down a one-way street when a policeman stopped him. The cop said, 'Didn't you see the arrows?' He said, 'Arrows? I didn't even see the Indians!'

I found a recipe for a hot toddy the other day. It said, 'Take a glass and half fill it with whiskey. Add sugar and lemon to taste, fill the glass with boiling water and place a candle at the foot of the bed. Drink the toddy until you can see three candles. Blow out the middle candle and go to sleep!'

A drunk walked into a bar with a parking meter under his arm. The bartender said, 'You can't bring that in here.' He said, 'I don't want to forget where I parked my car!'

One drunk said to another, 'I don't know what I've done or where I've been, but I wouldn't have missed it for the world!'

This fellow was so drunk he went inside the grandfather clock and tried to make a phone call!

A drunk was brought into a police station. He pounded his fist on the counter and said, 'I want to know why I've been arrested.' The sergeant said, 'You have been brought in for drinking.' He said, 'Oh, that's alright then. Let's get started!'

A drunk was passing a cemetery and saw the sign, 'Ring the bell for the caretaker.' He rang the bell and the caretaker came to the door and said, 'What do you want?' The drunk said, 'I want to know why you can't ring the bell for yourself.'

I'm beginning to realise that drink is a terrible thing. The other day I was in a bar and a big fight started. Chairs and tables were flying through the air. Beer bottles and knives were being thrown all over the place. Everything was being smashed. I would have jumped in and stopped it, but I didn't want to start any trouble!

It's often said that alcohol and petrol don't mix. They do, but it tastes terrible!

Drink and Drunks

I've been doing some research lately. I drank some whiskey and water and got drunk. Then I drank some brandy and water and got drunk again. Then I drank some rum and water and got drunk a third time. I've come to the conclusion that water must be intoxicating!

A lot of people can't sleep when they drink coffee. With me it's different ... when I sleep, I can't drink coffee!

I almost went blind drinking coffee ... I left the spoon in the cup!

I just had a Boy Scout Cocktail ... two of them and an old lady helps you across the street.

I know a bar where after the fifth drink they give you a test to see if you're sober. They draw a white line on the floor and if you don't trip over it, you're okay!

Two guys were standing at a bar drinking when all of a sudden one of them fell face down on the floor. His friend turned to the bartender and said, 'That's one good thing about him ... he always knows when to stop!'

He can't understand why the Russians don't like us. He takes two vodkas and likes everybody!

He drinks so much, when he blows on a birthday cake he lights the candles!

They say that drinking kills you slowly, but who's in a hurry?

A drunk came out of a nightclub and turned to the porter and yelled, 'Get me a cab.' This big man in uniform said, 'I'm sorry, young man ... I'm not a porter ... I'm an admiral.' The drunk said, 'Well alright then, call me a ship!'

What's the secret of your diet?
Peanut milk!
But how can you get milk from a peanut?
I use a very low stool!

Come down to the river and I'll show you a trick.
What kind of trick?
I'll jump in the water and stay under for three hours.
Three hours under water? You'll drown.
Oh, you know the trick!

Dreams

I had a terrible dream last night. I dreamt my wife and Jayne Mansfield were fighting and my wife was winning!

I had a wonderful dream last night. I dreamt that Brigitte Bardot came up to me and said, 'I will grant you three wishes. Now what are the other two?'

I can't get any sleep ... every time I go to bed I dream I'm awake!

I won't go to sleep for fear I'll dream I'm working!

I dreamt I was eating spaghetti. When I woke up, my pyjama cord had gone!

Last night I dreamt I was a cannon. When I woke up, I shot right out of bed!

Last night I dreamt I was eating a ten pound marshmallow. When I woke up, my pillow had gone!

Once I dreamt I was plucking a chicken. When I woke up, the wife was bald!

My brother used to work in the circus. They used to shoot him out of a cannon.

Was he hurt?

I don't know ... they never found him!

What kind of swimmer are you?

Well, I do the breaststroke for two hours and then I do the crawl for three hours.

And what do you do then?

Then I go in the water and wash the sand off!

You look down. What's bothering you?

I just feel lonely, so lonely that this morning I sat down and wrote myself a letter.

What did you say in it?

I don't know. I won't get it until tomorrow!

I swam the English Channel once.

But a lot of people have swum the Channel.

Lengthwise?

What a night I had! I kept seeing blue snakes and pink elephants.

Have you seen a doctor?

No, only blue snakes and pink elephants!

Take a card. Now I'll write the name of the card you picked on this piece of paper and I'll put it over here. Now think of your card. Got it? Now double it. Okay? Now add your weight. Now double that. Now add your height. Okay? Now divide the number in half. Right? Okay then, what's your card?

The 217 of clubs!

Double Gags

I used to juggle plates with one hand.
What did you do with the other hand?
Pick up the pieces!

It's my friend's birthday. I think I'll get him a gold cigarette lighter.
Do you know him that well?
Well, maybe I'll give him a silver lighter.
Is he that good a friend?
I know ... I'll get him a box of matches!

Hey, have you got a new five pound note for an old one?
I sure have.
(makes the exchange and Tommy turns to go)
Just a minute. This is only a one pound note.
I know ... I asked you for a new five pound note for an old one!

Why don't you go to a doctor? They give free operations.
I don't need anything taken out.
Well, have something put in!

I'll never forget the time I fell out of a plane.
That's bad.
Not too bad ... I had a parachute.
That's good.
Not too good ... the parachute didn't open.
That's bad.
Not too bad ... there was a big haystack on the ground below.
That's good.
Not too good ... there was a pitchfork sticking up.
That's bad.
Not too bad ... I missed the pitchfork.
That's good.
Not too good ... I missed the haystack!

Do-It-Yourself

My wife is really into Do-It-Yourself. Every time I ask her to fix something, she says, 'Oh, do it yourself!'

My wife does her own decorating, but she overdoes it. The other day I opened the fridge and there was a lamp shade on the light bulb.

Have you heard of those portable home kits? I must have done something wrong. Every time I walked out the front door, I fell off the roof!

My uncle was a farmer and he had an old sheep dog. I swear that dog understood every word he said. One day I said to my uncle, 'I swear that dog understands every word you say.' He said, 'Woof, woof!'

I have a sheep dog. Some dogs have fleas ... this one has moths!

Here's to the dog who walked up to a tree
That said to the dog, 'Have one on me!'
But the dog replied, as meek as a mouse,
'No thanks, dear tree. I just had one on the house!'

This fellow took his dog to a theatrical agent and told him the dog could sing and dance and tell jokes. After the audition the agent was so impressed he booked the dog immediately for the London Palladium. While the dog was doing his act, a big dog rushed in, grabbed him and pulled him off the stage. The producer asked the owner what happened and the owner said, 'Oh, that's his mother. She wants him to be a doctor!'

This guy got onto a train and sat opposite an old lady who had a little dog on her lap. It had so much hair, you couldn't tell one end from the other. As soon as he sat down the dog jumped off the lady's lap and bit him on the ankle. The guy didn't say a word. He just put his hand in his pocket and produced a biscuit, which he put on the floor for the dog. The old lady was amazed. She said, 'My word! You are a kind man. My little dog bites you on the ankle and you give him a biscuit.' He said, 'I'm not being kind. I put the biscuit on the floor to find out which end he eats from. Then I can kick the other!'

I bought my wife a lapdog, but she got rid of it. Every time she sat on the dog's lap, it bit her!

I asked the vet why my dog chased cars. He said, 'That's only natural. Most dogs chase cars.' I said, 'I know, but mine catches them and buries them in the garden!'

C
D

I said, 'Doctor, I keep thinking I'm a camera.' He said, 'You'll just have to snap out of it!'

I said, 'Doctor, I keep getting these dizzy spells.' He said, 'Vertigo?' I said, 'No, I only live up the road!'

The doctor said, 'How did you hurt yourself?' I said, 'I was up on the roof and I happened to bend down to tie up my shoelaces.' He said, 'How can you hurt yourself that way?' I said, 'My shoes were down on the ground!'

Dogs

I've got a one-man dog ... he only bites me!

I bought a watchdog ... but someone stole the dog!

I sent him to one of those obedience schools and now every time I say, 'Heel,' that's where he bites me!

I've got a dog that can read. The other day it walked past a sign that said 'Wet paint.' He did just what the sign said!

A dog bit a chunk out of my leg the other day. A friend of mine said, 'Did you put anything on it?' I said, 'No, he liked it as it was!'

My dog is harmless really. I say to him, 'Attack!' and he has one!

I've got a very smart dog. All you have to say is, 'Are you coming or not?' and he either comes or he doesn't!

My dog must have belonged to a waiter. He never comes when I call him!

I used to do a dog act. It was so bad the critics used to say that if the dog had any brains he'd do a single.

Doctors

I went to see my doctor today. He hasn't been feeling well lately!

My doctor told me to drink a bottle of wine after a hot bath, but I couldn't even finish drinking the hot bath!

I went to the doctor today for a check-up and he said I'm lucky ... if I was a building, I'd be condemned!

A doctor went into the waiting room and found a man with scratches all over his arms, his clothes all torn to shreds and a pelican standing on his head. The doctor said, 'Well, sir, what can I do for you?' The pelican said, 'How can I get this thing off my feet?'

An old man went to the doctor for a check-up and when the doctor finished examining him, he said to the old man, 'You're in good shape. You'll live to be eighty.' The old guy said, 'But I am eighty.' The doctor said, 'See, what did I tell you?'

The doctor said, 'I hope you've been eating lots of fruit with their skins on.' I said, 'Well actually it hasn't been agreeing with me.' He said, 'What have you been eating?' I said, 'Pineapples, coconuts and bananas!'

The doctor said, 'Do you suffer from rheumatism or arthritis?' I said, 'Do you know anybody who enjoys it?'

I said to my doctor the other day, 'One of my legs is shorter than the other. What shall I do?' He said, 'Limp!'

I said, 'Doctor, I keep thinking I'm a monkey wrench.' He said, 'For goodness sake, try and get a grip on yourself!'

I said, 'Doctor, I keep thinking I'm a pair of curtains.' He said, 'Well pull yourself together!'

C
D

I know a guy who took just one slimming pill and lost nine pounds ... his arm fell off!

If you want to lose weight, try skipping ... skipping lunch ... skipping dinner ... !

I know a guy who lost so much weight, even his cufflinks don't fit him any more!

Have you heard about the new four day diet? On the first day you cut out liquids ... on the second day you cut out food ... on the third day you cut out smoking ... and on the fourth day you cut out paper dolls!

I went to a health farm and the first week they gave me nothing to eat. I lost five pounds ... a guy took a bite out of my shoulder!

Divorce

Henny Youngman tells of an eighty-year-old woman who was suing her husband after sixty-two years of marriage. The judge said, 'And you want a divorce now?' She said, 'Yes. Enough is enough!'

I read where a marriage broke up so fast, the bride got custody of the wedding cake!

This woman said, 'Your honour, my husband has beaten me every day for the past year. I'm such a nervous wreck I've lost thirty pounds.' He said, 'And you want a divorce?' She said, 'Yes, but I want to lose another eight pounds first!'

He spent so much time in the doghouse, he finally got his divorce through the RSPCA!

He's so healthy, he's got a different dentist for every tooth!

Dieting

There's only one way to diet ... watch your food! Don't eat it. Just watch it!

They've just discovered a new slimming pill. It paralyses your mouth so you can't eat!

When I went on a diet, I ate so much lettuce rabbits were calling me by my first name!

I've lost so much weight, even my shoelaces don't fit!

I'm on a seafood diet ... whenever I see food, I eat it!

I'm on a strict diet ... only one breakfast, lunch and dinner per day!

I'm on a whiskey diet ... last week I lost three days!

I went on an onion diet. I lost ten pounds and twelve friends!

I went on a champagne diet ... in six weeks I lost a thousand pounds!

He lost so much weight, even his toupee looks baggy!

For ten days my wife ate nothing but dog biscuits. She didn't lose any weight, but she's barking much better!

My wife went on a diet of coconuts and bananas. She lost twenty pounds ... just by swinging from chandelier to chandelier!

She's on a diet now. She eats nothing but coconuts and bananas. She hasn't lost any weight, but you should see her climb trees!

Death

Two guys were walking down the street. One said, 'Did you know that Sam died?' The other said, 'No ... did he leave anything?' He said, 'Yes ... everything!'

This old man was sinking fast and as he lay there unconscious, his sons gathered round his bedside to make the arrangements for his funeral. The first one said, 'I can get thirty carriages to the cemetery for a thousand pounds.' The second said, 'We don't need that many carriages. I can get ten for three hundred pounds.' The third son said, 'Now wait a minute, guys. A funeral is only a symbol. We only need five carriages and I can get them for eighty.' The old man opened one eye and said, 'If you'll get me my trousers, I'll get up and walk to the cemetery!'

My aunt died recently and gave me this diamond ring to remember her by. Just look at that sparkle! Just before she died, she said, 'Here's five hundred pounds ... buy the best stone you can find!'

Dentists

I'm always afraid when I go to the dentist. I need an anaesthetic just to sit in the waiting room.

When I asked the dentist to put a cap on my tooth, he put a hat on it!

I always wanted to be a dentist, but my hands were too big. Before I could get to the back teeth I had to pull out all the front teeth.

A woman and her husband went into the dentist's. She said, 'I want a tooth out and I don't want gas because I'm in a dreadful hurry. Just pull the tooth out as quickly as possible so I can be on my way.' The dentist said, 'You're very brave. Which tooth is it?' She turned to her husband and said, 'Get in the chair and show the dentist which tooth.'

D is for Dog

C
D

A terrorist hijacked a bus full of Japanese tourists and stole all their jewellery. But the police say they should catch him fairly quickly ... they have three thousand photos of him!

A fellow was telling a friend about his three wives and what became of them. He said, 'The first one died of mushrooms, the second one also died of mushrooms, but the third one died from a fractured skull.' He said, 'How was that?' He said, 'She wouldn't eat the mushrooms!'

Three kids were brought before the juvenile court for disturbing the peace. The judge turned to the first one and said, 'What are you here for?' He said, 'Just for throwing peanuts in the water.' The judge said, 'Well, that doesn't seem such a terrible thing,' turned to the second boy and asked him the same question. He said, 'I threw peanuts in the water too.' The judge then turned to the third boy and said, 'And I suppose you threw peanuts in the water also?' He said, 'No, your honour. I am Peanuts!'

I was minding my own business when a fellow came up and poked a gun in my back. He said, 'Stick 'em up!' I said, 'Stick what up?' He said, 'Don't confuse me ... I'm new on the job!'

Customs

A woman was passing through customs. The customs officer said, 'Are you sure, madam, you have nothing to declare?' She said, 'Yes ... absolutely nothing.' He said, 'You mean that the fur tail hanging down from under your dress is your own?'

We had a wonderful candlelight supper. She makes the most delicious candles!

I gave her a bottle of bath salts for her birthday. When I asked her how she liked them, she said, 'Oh, they tasted nice, but I don't think they have the same effect as a real bath!'

Cowboys

You've heard of the Lone Ranger ... I'm his brother, Hydrangea!

I figured out why Zorro rides only at night. He hasn't finished paying for his horse yet!

You know why a cowboy dies with his boots on? So he won't hurt himself when he kicks the bucket!

Crime

The other day I was standing in Piccadilly Circus when I felt a hand in my pocket. I yelled at the guy, 'What's the big idea?' He said, 'I was just looking for a match.' I said, 'Why didn't you ask?' He said, 'Because I don't talk to strangers!'

I knew him well ... we have the same probation officer!

(as Sherlock Holmes:) 'I say, Watson, this is a most serious case ... the window is broken on both sides.'

(as the judge to the beautiful, blonde defendant:) 'Now tell the Jury in your own words how you accidentally happened to stab your husband six times!'

The first cop said, 'Didn't you guard the exits?' The other one said, 'Yes ... he must have got out of one of the entrances.'

Cooking

I miss my wife's cooking ... every chance I get!

She used to go to cookery school, but they threw her out ... she burnt the school!

To cook rice so it won't stick together ... boil it one grain at a time!

I've got a great recipe for pot roast. First brown the roast, then add a fifth of vodka, two quarts of gin, four shots of tequila, a jigger of whiskey, three tablespoons of champagne and then cook for an hour and a half. When it's done ... well, the roast is nothing, but the gravy's delicious!

I won't say she's a lousy cook, but who heard of boiling sardines?

I said to the chef, 'Why have you got your hand in the alphabet soup?' He said, 'I'm groping for words!'

Courtship

When I asked her to whisper those three little words that would make me walk on air, she said, 'Sure ... go hang yourself!'

Her boy friend gave her a big ring ... it holds twenty keys!

Was I surprised when she put her head on my shoulder! I didn't know it came off!

I took her to the pictures and we held hands all through the film. It would have been better if our seats had been together!

I took her to the pictures and it was so exciting, she sat on the edge of her seat all through the movie. She had to. I only bought one ticket!

Do you know why a polar bear wears a fur coat? It would look stupid in tweed!

I surprised my wife with a mink coat. She'd never seen me in one before!

I said to my wife, 'You look just like you looked the day we were married twenty years ago.' She said, 'I should do. It's the same dress!'

I said, 'I know a person who never wears a shirt or a tie but is always well dressed.' She said, 'Who's that?' I said, 'My mother!'

Coffee

I said, 'Waiter, take this coffee away. It tastes like mud.' He said, 'It should do. It was ground only this morning!'

Comedy

Once I took a correspondence course on how to become a comedian. It was supposed to come in ten easy lessons, but I only received the first and the last. I don't know what happened to the other eight, but my postman is playing the Palladium!

Commercials

What I can't work out is how every car, toothpaste and cereal can be better than every other car, toothpaste and cereal?

'Try the new deodorant called "Disappear". After you rub it on once or twice, you will disappear and nobody will know where the smell is coming from!'

'Try our cough mixture ... you'll never get better!'

It said in the newspaper, 'Do your Christmas shopping early.' So I got up at five o'clock this morning, but all the shops were closed!

C
D

All I expect for Christmas is my wife's relations!
And what is the best description of Santa Clause? A blessing in disguise!

Circus

I used to do a juggling act with fifteen clubs, twenty plates and thirty rubber balls. I finally had to give it up. I couldn't figure out what to do with the other hand!

I love the sideshows in the circus. I once saw the tallest man in the world. He was so tall that if he ever fell over he'd have been out of town.

My wife said, 'If you were half a man, you'd take me to the circus ...
I said, 'If I were half a man, I'd be in the circus!'

Clothes

This morning I thought the laundry had sent me the wrong shirt. The collar was so tight I could hardly breathe. Then I found out I had my head through a buttonhole!

If you ever saw me in a bathing suit ... I look like a potato with legs!

Boy, you should have seen her dress! I didn't know if she was in that dress trying to get out or outside trying to get in!

My tailor said, 'You're putting on a bit of weight. Why don't you wear a corset?' I said, 'Wear a corset?' He said, 'Yes, that'll pull your stomach in, a corset will.' I said, 'A corset will?' He said, 'O' course it will!'

A little boy got a watch for his birthday. Someone said, 'That's a pretty watch you've got there ... does it tell you the time?' He said, 'No, this is an old-fashioned watch ... you have to look at it!'

Christmas

I bought my little boy one of those unbreakable toys. It cost me a fortune. He broke every other toy in the house with it!

One Christmas I got a job as Santa Claus in a department store. One little girl sat on my knee and said, 'Guess what I've got.' I said, 'A doll?' She said, 'No.' I said, 'A Christmas list?' She said, 'No.' I said, 'I give up. What have you got?' She said, 'Chickenpox!'

I just finished my Christmas shopping. I bought an electric train set, a scooter, a space helmet and a Meccano set, and I also got some things for the kids.

I said to the girl in the shop, 'I want to give my wife half of a ping pong table for Christmas.' She said, 'Why half a table?' I said, 'She doesn't play!'

Don't forget ... a useful Christmas gift is one that can be exchanged!

C
D

I used to be afraid of the dark, so my mother always put a lighted candle next to my bed ... now I'm afraid of candles!

I said to my mother, 'Can I go out and play with the child next door?' She said, 'No. You know I don't like the kid next door.' I said, 'Then can I go out and beat the hell out of him?'

One Sunday I came home with my pockets full of cash. My mother said, 'Where did you get that?' I said, 'In church ... they've got plates full of it there!'

My teacher said, 'If there are any idiots in the class, please stand up.' After a while I got up. He said, 'Do you consider yourself an idiot?' I said, 'No ... I just hated to see you standing alone!'

When we were kids we were so tough we used to have pillow fights with bags of nails!

Children

My kids sit and watch television in the living room all day. It's got me worried. Our set is in the bedroom!

The other day my little boy came running up to me shouting, 'Mother has just run over my bicycle while she was backing out of the garage.' I said, 'How many times have I told you not to leave your bike on the front porch?'

The trouble with kids today is they get spoiled too fast. I spent twenty pounds on a space suit for my little boy and then he wouldn't go.

A little boy was standing on a street corner with a cigarette in his mouth and a glass of whiskey in his hand. An old lady came by and said, 'Sonny, why aren't you at school?' He said, 'Because I'm only three!'

I came from a very poor family of five children. We all used to sleep in the same bed. In fact, I never slept alone until I got married.

I never had any luck as a kid. I had a rocking horse once that died!

I had a lead pencil that leaked!

One birthday my father bought me a bat. When I went to play with it, it flew away!

I was different from the kids who were six or seven years old ... I was ten!

I was born with a silver spoon in my mouth ... all the other kids had tongues!

We were so poor my mother used to buy me one shoe at a time.

When I was two I memorised the entire encyclopaedia, but no one believed me because I couldn't talk!

When my father was through explaining about the birds and the bees, he said, 'Are there any questions?' I said, 'Yes ... how can a leopard tell when he's got the measles?'

When I was a kid my father used to give me a penny every day and then he'd pat me on the head. By the time I was fifteen I had twenty quid and a flat head!

My teacher used to tell me that two and two made four. The next day she told me that one and three made four. She never made up her mind!

I came home from school one day and told my father I needed an encyclopaedia. He said, 'Encyclopaedia, my eye! You'll walk to school like everyone else.'

Childhood

Childhood is that wonderful time when all you have to do to lose weight is to take a bath!

I was a big surprise to my parents. They found me on the doorstep. They were expecting a bottle of milk!

When the nurse told my mother she had an eight pound bundle of joy, she said, 'Thank God, the laundry's back!'

Caerphilly in Wales is the healthiest place in the country. When I first came there I couldn't say a word, I didn't have a single hair on my head and I didn't have the strength to walk across the room. How long was I there? I was born there!

When I was born I was so tough ... when the doctor slapped me, I slapped him back!

When I was a baby I had the cutest little button nose, but they couldn't feed me ... it was buttoned to my lower lip!

I was so shy as a kid, when I was born I was three years old!

I wasn't sure whether my parents disliked me until I came home from school one day and found out they had moved!

C
D

One day she said to me, 'I don't want to upset you, but I've got a slight scratch on the bumper.' I asked her to show it to me. She said, 'It's in the boot!'

Last night she backed the car out of the garage perfectly. That would have been okay, but she had just backed it in!

This cop stopped me and said, 'You were doing ninety miles an hour.' I said, 'Don't be silly, officer. This car can't run for an hour!'

Two friends both bought their wives new small cars. When they were delivered, they stood and admired them. One of them lifted the bonnet of her car to see the tiny motor she had heard so much about, but she couldn't see it. She said, 'Mabel, look, they've forgotten to put the motor in my car.' Mabel said, 'Don't worry. I was looking in the boot of my car and I found one there. They must have given me an extra one, so I'll give you one of mine!'

I call my car 'Flattery' ... it gets me nowhere!

Chickens

A man ordered a crate of live chickens. When the farmer delivered them there was no one home, so he left them on the front porch. When the guy came back, the crate was empty and he had to run all over the neighbourhood to catch them. He then rang the farmer. He said, 'Do you know it took me three hours to round them up and I could only find sixteen.' The farmer said, 'What are you complaining about ... I only delivered eight!'

I was walking down the street the other day and I looked over this fence and there was a little chicken, a little Rhode Island Red, and it looked up and went, 'Cluck, cluck.' So I went, 'Cluck, cluck.' And then it went, 'Cluck, cluck' again and I went, 'Cluck, cluck.' Then this policeman came along and arrested us for using foul language!

Cannibals

They say a cannibal is a guy who loves his fellow man – with gravy!

Did you hear of the cannibal who ate a missionary? He wanted a taste of religion!

The cannibal said, 'My wife made a wonderful pot roast. I'm going to miss her!'

Cars

They've developed a new car ... no clutch, no brakes and no motor. There's only one snag. They can't drive it out of the factory!

When you're driving at night and you see a car coming towards you, dim your headlights. If you can't dim your headlights, turn the radio up real loud!

I got a ticket for parking today ... I haven't even got a car!

I've only had my car three months, but I'll have to buy a new one ... the ashtrays are full!

I bought a car the other day. I said to the guy at the garage, 'All the tyres are flat.' He said, 'Yes, but only at the bottom!'

My wife doesn't really park a car ... she abandons it!

One day my wife came in and said, 'I've got some good news.' I said, 'What's that?' She said, 'You haven't been paying those premiums on the car for nothing!'

Every day she takes the car out, she comes back with the same question ... 'Guess who I ran into?'

C is for Cowboy

This fighter sat in his corner between the ninth and last round. His manager said, 'I'm afraid this guy's got you licked.' The fighter looked at his opponent through his half-closed eyes and said, 'Yes, I should have got him in the first round when he was by himself!'

This fighter was knocked to the floor and the referee started the count. When he got to 'Four', his manager shouted, 'Don't get up till "Eight".' He looked up and said, 'Okay, what time is it now?'

My best punch was a rabbit punch, but they wouldn't let me fight rabbits.

I'm in good shape. I can still go ten rounds as long as someone is buying them!

Building

A foreman at a big building site collared one of the workmen and said, 'Hey! How come you're only carrying four bricks at a time, when the others are carrying eight?' He said, 'Well, I guess they're just plain lazy. They're not prepared to make two trips like I do!'

Business

Buddy Hackett has this description of a millionaire friend who got fifty million dollars to sell out his business with the understanding that he wasn't to go into the same business again. So he bought the bank that held the mortgage on the business, then he foreclosed the mortgage and now he's got the business back again!

I just made a terrific deal. I bought up all the heat in town and I'm storing it away till the winter!

This boxer got a terrible beating in the first round. He staggered to his corner and the manager whispered, 'You won that round.' He got a terrible beating in the second, third and fourth rounds as well and every time the manager said, 'You won that round.' The fifth round was the same ... he was massacred. He staggered back to his corner and the manager said, 'Attaboy, you won that round too.' The boxer said, 'Then tell the referee to give him the next five rounds and call it a draw!'

Books

I saw a sign in a book shop that read, 'Newly translated from the French ... 27 Mating Positions.' When I got home, it was a book about chess!

I love Shakespeare. I read all his books ... as soon as they come out!

Boxing

I have a photo of myself in the days when I was a boxer. If you turn it sideways it looks as if I'm standing up!

They used to call me Canvasback Cooper. I used to go into the ring vertical and come out horizontal!

They used to call me Rembrandt ... I was always on the canvas!

I did pretty good at the beginning. I won my first ten fights. Then I ran into trouble ... they made me fight a man!

She had her face lifted so many times, now she talks through her eyes!

She uses pancake make-up ... real pancakes with syrup!

She's always smiling ... she's the only girl I know whose teeth are sunburnt!

She had her face lifted so many times, it's out of focus!

Bequest

This old man was dying and he called his nephew to his bedside. He said, 'I'm leaving you all my money.' The nephew said, 'Thank you, uncle. What can I do for you?' He said, 'Get your foot off my oxygen tube!'

Birds

The early bird catches the worm ... but who wants worms?

Fred Allen used to talk about the bird that flew backwards because it didn't care where it was going ... it was only interested in where it had been. I've got a bird that flies upside down ... if it's shot by a hunter it will fall up instead of down!

Fred Allen knew a farmer who had a scarecrow that scared crows so badly, they brought back corn they had taken two years before!

A man walked into a pet shop and saw a beautiful bird that not only sang beautifully, but also spoke seven different languages. He bought the bird and had it sent home. When he got home later in the day, he said to his wife, 'Did you get the bird I sent home earlier?' She said, 'Yes, I've got it in the oven now.' He said, 'What? In the oven? That bird speaks seven different languages!' She said, 'Well, why didn't he say something?'

Barbers

I went into a barber's shop and said, 'How much is a hair cut?' He said, 'Ten pounds.' I said, 'How much is a shave?' He said, 'A fiver.' I said, 'Shave my head!'

A fellow walked into a barber's shop and asked for a shave. This new assistant barber was doing nothing and said, 'How about letting me shave him, boss? It will be good practice.' The boss said, 'Okay, go ahead. But be careful ... don't cut yourself!'

I was telling my barber how I was planning a trip to Italy on one of these economy flights. He said, 'You don't want to do that. The plane will be crowded, the heat is terrible and besides if you think you'll get in to see the Pope, you can forget it.' Three months later I was back in the same barber's. I told him the trip was terrific, the plane was very comfortable and the weather was just right. He said, 'Okay, but did you get in to see the Pope?' I said, 'Yes, and what is more I got a private audience.' He said, 'And what did the Pope say?' I said, 'He said, "Where did you get that lousy haircut?"'

Bathing Beauty

I love bathing beauties, but the trouble is I never bathe any!

Beauty

My wife went to a beauty parlour for a mud pack. It looked so good on her, she wore it for three days!

She has such beautiful unusual lips ... both on top!

She had plastic surgery done on her nose. She had it moved between her eyes!

All those girls dancing round on their toes ... if they want taller girls, why don't they get them?

My wife said, 'How did you enjoy the ballet?' I said, 'I couldn't hear a word they were saying!'

I've tiptoed into my house so many times at four in the morning, the neighbours think I'm a ballet dancer!

I used to be a ballet dancer. I was priceless in 'Swan Lake' and matchless in Swan Vestas!

Only two things prevented me becoming a dancer myself ... *my feet!*

Banana

Two fellows were on a train. One took out a banana and started to eat it, peel and all. The other said, 'What are you doing? Why don't you peel the banana before you eat it?' The other said, 'Why? I know what's inside.'

Bank

A woman went to the bank to cash a cheque. The cashier said, 'Can you identify yourself?' She took a mirror out of her handbag, looked into it and said, 'Yes, it's me!'

Barbecue

There's a guy having a barbecue in his front garden. He's turning the spit like this and the flames are getting higher and higher – higher and higher – and he's singing, 'Oh sole mio ... O sole mio, farewell.' And the flames are getting higher and higher and this drunk walks by and says, 'Your singing's alright, but your monkey's on fire!'

Bachelor

This bachelor was forty years old and still living at home. His friend said, 'You ought to get yourself a girl.' He said, 'I know, but whatever girl I take home, my mother disapproves.' The friend said, 'Why don't you find a girl just like your mother, then she's bound to like her.' A few months later the bachelor met the friend again and told him he had followed his advice. He said, 'I finally found a girl just like my mother. She looked like my mother, she talked like my mother and she even cooked like my mother.' The friend said, 'So what happened?' He said, 'My father hated her!'

Baker

A guy went into a baker's shop and asked the baker to bake him a cake in the shape of a letter 'K'. The baker told him to come back in a week and the cake would be ready. A week later he went back and saw the cake. He said, 'I'm sorry, but you misunderstood me. I wanted it made in the shape of a small letter "k", not a capital letter "K".' Another week went by and he went back to the shop again. This time he was delighted with the result. The baker said, 'Will you take it with you, sir?' The man said, 'No. Just give me a knife and fork and I'll eat it here!'

Balaclava

Balaclava? I don't know any jokes about a balaclava!

Ballet

My wife wanted to go to the ballet. I said, 'I'm not going to sit and watch a lot of people on their toes in long underwear.' She said, 'You don't have to. Wear your tuxedo.'

B is for Balaclava

I'll never forget the night I made my first appearance as a comedian ... don't think I haven't tried!

Why am I working so fast? I've got the job!

I don't exactly steal jokes ... I just find them before other comedians realise they're missing!

All these jokes are insured against failure, so please laugh or I'll lose my no claims bonus!

That was my best joke ... from here on, it's nerve!

Last night I had an audience! Laugh? I thought they'd never start!

Be patient. My act usually starts slowly ... and then generally peters out!

Audition

A man turned up at an audition and was asked what he could do. He said, 'I do bird impressions.' The producer said, 'Don't waste my time. I don't want any bird imitators on my show.' He said, 'Sorry I bothered you' and flew out of the window.

Australia

A Texan was being shown round this huge farm in Australia. He said, 'This would fit into a small corner of my ranch back in Texas.' Then the Australian showed him his thousands of head of cattle and the Texan said, 'Why, they'd get lost among my herd!' Just then a kangaroo leaped by and the Texan shouted, 'What the hell is that?' The Australian said, 'You mean to tell me you don't have grasshoppers in Texas?'

TOMMY COOPER'S

One night I was doing my act and the whole audience got up and started dancing. And the music wasn't even playing!

After the show we're going to have a competition. You must send in twenty-five words or less on 'Why I like Tommy Cooper.' All entries must be written on a twenty pound note!

Last night I had the audience on their feet ... there was a mouse running up and down the aisle!

I don't have to do this for a living ... but who wants to go back to plucking chickens?

It's not generally known, but one in every four people is a nutcase. So get three friends together and if they're all right ... it's you!

I almost didn't make it here tonight. I had a terrible accident. I fell off the ironing board. I was pressing my trousers and I forgot to take them off!

Now I would like to leave you with an old Norwegian saying, 'Svensky in potorskey ghebin novoja.' I don't know what it means ... I read it on the back of a tin of sardines once.

(when you stumble over a line) How about that? I had my nose fixed, and now my mouth won't work!

Please be quiet. I've got a sleeping pill in my hand and I don't want to wake it up!

I'm so nervous tonight, I'm afraid I'll say something funny!

If you're in a hurry, don't worry. I've got a pretty fast act ... before you get a chance to hate me, I'll be gone!

Audience Lines

Yes, I know ... I'm crazy – but you paid!

(after applause) Goodness, am I that good? I want more money!

And now for those who came in late ... aren't you glad?

(to a bad audience) I've died in better coffins than this!

Please don't applaud ... it creates a draught!

Any time you want me here again, just say the word ... money!

Well, how do you like that ... a sitting ovation!

You know, these jokes could be worse ... they could be mine!

I'm so confident tonight, I didn't even wear my good suit!

Don't applaud ... I'll lose my place!

I don't care what you think ... I'm staying in show business!

I'd like to say something funny, but I don't want to break the spell!

What a lovely audience ... I'll do the full act tonight! I won't cut a thing!

What an audience! I had them eating out of my hand. They must have thought they were at the zoo!

Art

I know he's a sculptor ... I heard someone say, 'There goes that dirty chiseller!'

I did her portrait in oils ...
she has a face like a sardine!

Once I painted a girl in the nude and I almost froze to death!

Anybody can paint oranges ...
I paint the juice!

Asides

Do you think I'm too handsome for my height?

He who laughs last usually has a tooth missing!

After all, what are rich people? Just poor people with money!

I always call a spade a spade, until the other night when I stepped on one in the dark!

Atlantic

This fellow was paddling across the Atlantic in a bathtub when the captain of a liner saw him and yelled out, 'What are you doing?' He said, 'I'm sailing to America.' The captain said, 'You must be crazy. This ocean is very dangerous.' He said, 'I know, but I'm hurrying to catch up with my brother. He's trying to cross in a frying pan!'

A
B

A fellow saw a man coming towards him with an animal on his shoulder. He said, 'Hey, are you a monkey or a chimp?' The animal said, 'I'm a chimp.' And the fellow said, 'I wasn't talking to you!'

A rabbit and a lion went into a restaurant and the rabbit ordered a head of lettuce with no dressing. The waiter said, 'And what will your friend have?' The rabbit said, 'Nothing. He isn't hungry. If he were, do you think I'd be sitting here?'

A man ran over a hare, so he stopped his car, got out and gave the hare a swig from a hip flask. All of a sudden the hare jumped up and ran off into the bushes. His friend said, 'That's amazing! What the hell have you got in that flask?' The man said, 'Hare restorer!'

Antiques

I said, 'You remember that Napoleon bathtub you sold me? Well, I think Napoleon is still in it!' He said, 'Don't be silly. Napoleon's been dead for over a hundred years.' I said, 'Then who's scratching my back?'

Now here's a quick laugh. Do this tomorrow. Walk into an antique shop and shout, 'What's new?'

Army

In the last war I fought and fought ... but I had to go anyway!

If you want to stay out of the army ... join the navy!

I only just avoided a court martial. I was assigned to the officers' party and told to stand at the door and call the officers' names!'

Agents

If you want to get on in show business, you've got to have an agent.
In fact, I've got two ... they're double agents!

My agent is a great bloke. Well, without him I wouldn't be working here
today ... I'd have retired ten years ago!

Alarm Clock

A woman rushed into the hospital with her little boy and said, 'Doctor,
my little boy has swallowed an alarm clock.' He said, 'An alarm clock?
Does it bother him?' She said, 'It doesn't bother him, but it bothers me.'
He said, 'Why?' She said, 'Well, every time I go to wind it up, he bites
my finger.'

Alphabet

My little boy learnt the alphabet. I said, 'What comes after A?' He said,
'All the rest of them!'

Animals

A fellow kept his pet mice in the top drawer of his dresser and kept some
cheese in the bottom drawer. His friend said, 'How do you stop the mice
from getting at the cheese?' He said, 'Oh, in the middle drawer I keep
my cat.'

One day I was drinking some milk and a cow fell on me!

Two sheep were together in the meadow when one of them went, 'Baa-
aa.' The other sheep went, 'Moo-oo.' The first one said, 'Moo? What's this
"Moo" bit?' and the second one said, 'I'm taking up a foreign language!'

Absent-Minded

I used to be very absent-minded, so one night I took a piece of paper and wrote on it, 'Shirt in the wardrobe ... tie on the tie rack ... trousers on the chair ... shoes and socks on the floor' ... and then I went to sleep. The next morning when I got up everything was where it should have been. My shoes and socks were on the floor, my trousers were on the chair, my tie was on the tie rack and my shirt was in the wardrobe. Then I looked at the bed and I wasn't there!

Actor-Cannons

See Introduction: page 10

After-Dinner Speaking

He's a great after-dinner speaker. He's always on the phone when the waiter brings the bill!

How to make a successful speech: Get up! Speak up! Shut up! Sit down!

When I came here today I had a beautiful speech all prepared and only God and I knew what I was going to say. Now I can't find it and God only knows!

I'm always nervous before getting up to make a speech, but as soon as I hear my own voice, I'm reassured!

The greatest after-dinner speech of them all is 'Put it all on one bill and don't hand it to me!'

One way to shorten after-dinner speeches would be to have them before dinner!

Today we're pleased to have as a speaker a man who has a train to catch in fifteen minutes!

A is for Army

sheets that he never got around to entering in his A-Z index. Some of them have now found their intended destination. I have also taken the liberty of sometimes rephrasing a joke if the voice in my head has told me that doing so would have better suited his delivery. My own selection process has been helped – and made all the more enjoyable – by the simple device of reading through his files with that unmistakable voice in one's ears, a sound he himself likened to 'combing a wire-haired terrier against the grain'! For maximum pleasure readers are asked to follow the same course.

'Tommy Cooper's Secret Joke Files' are being published in what would have been the year of his ninetieth birthday, twenty-seven years after his death on live television on 15 April 1984. Tucked away in the pages that follow is a joke that has an especially poignant subtext in that respect:

TV

```
I always had trouble getting on TV.  I even offered
to kill myself on TV.  It would be a real first!
```

He never meant it that way, of course, just as he never meant to leave us at the moment he did with so many jokes untold and so many tricks still to be tried. Since his death both his persona and his material have passed into the stuff of folklore to an extent that has eluded his comedy contemporaries. He would never have envisaged it that way. By his own modest interpretation he saw himself as a comparative amateur up against the likes of Benny Hill, Frankie Howerd and Morecambe & Wise and always swore they were far funnier than he was. To ensure he kept up with them he had to work hard and, figuratively speaking, stay on his toes. As this is being written, a poll has just been published in which Cooper has been credited with no less than thirteen of the top fifty jokes of all time, more than any other comedian, with five in the top ten alone and poll position to boot. The following pages will enable the reader to look over Tommy's shoulder as he stared much of his material in the face for the first hard time and confronted the challenge of staying in the comedy race, oblivious of the fact that in another lifetime he would prove to be the undisputed winner by miles.

Cold War and Vietnam, even though topicality was never a concern of Cooper's humour, a stance that provides one of the reasons why his spoken comedy still works today. However, to maintain the colour of the original, no effort has been made in this volume to update references to dance crazes, sex symbols or political scapegoats of the time where their meaning will still be understood. In some cases today's reality has rendered yesterday's jokes less funny than they might have been when first devised. The unintended presentiment makes them no less interesting and a few examples have been included for curiosity's sake, as with

PARKING

```
The parking situation is still so tough that some
guys are carrying bicycles in their cars to get to and
from parking places!
```

and

BUSINESS

```
I've just made a terrific deal. I bought up all the heat
in town and I'm storing it away till the WINTER!
(A GOOD SUMMER GAG)
```

Only very occasionally would a joke be credited in the joke bulletins to its original American practitioner, but on those occasions Cooper carried over the credit, with the result that comedy legends like Fred Allen, Jack Benny, Milton Berle, Buddy Hackett and Henny Youngman make cameo appearances in the pages that follow.

It is possible in the space available to feature only a fraction of the material Cooper set in store for comedy's rainy day. For the sake of simplicity, I have discarded his occasional distinction between 'P' and '1-L' material. That speaks for itself on the printed page. In some cases I have re-categorised jokes to make the text more user-friendly and even added new categories, as, for example, with 'D for Dog,' where previously all the 'Dog' jokes were listed under 'A for Animal.' Tommy also sometimes marked gags on the joke

became

I said, 'Waiter, this chicken's got one leg shorter than the other.' He said, 'What do you want to do? Eat it or dance with it?'

Since the wealth of the material at Cooper's disposal in this way originated in the United States, it was not surprising that occasionally a major cultural shift would be called for. Take, for example,

```
A Beatnik in Greenwich Village rigged up a do-it-yourself
   charcoal grill on his fire-escape and put a chicken
   on it to broil, when he heard one of his Beatnik
   pals yell up "Hey Dad, I don t wanna bug ya, but
   your music box has stopped and your monkey is on
   fire!"
```

The text is almost unrecognisable as the classic Cooper gem it became. Translated to London suburbia and transplanted to his act the joke became transformed as follows.

There's a guy having a barbecue in his front garden. He's turning the spit like this and the flames are getting higher and higher – higher and higher – and he's singing, 'O sole mio ... O sole mio, farewell.' And the flames are getting higher and higher and this drunk walks by and says, 'Your singing's alright, but your monkey's on fire!'

He had to be ever alert to the need for Anglicisation, although he was happy to include in his index categories for quintessentially American subjects like Thanksgiving, Drug Store, Dude Ranch, Democrat, Miami (as a holiday destination) - topics he knew he could always work around to his own more localised ends. As if to tell us that the period when he was active in this regard bridged the mid-fifties to the early seventies, he even compiled his own cache of jokes appertaining to the Brain Drain, the Space Race, the *jungle?' And he hit the ground hard. And he picked him up again and he threw him against the tree and he threw him against the other tree. Then the other one. Then the other one. Then the other one. And he sank to the ground like that. It may have been like that. No. It was like that. And the lion said to the elephant, 'Look, there's no good getting mad just because you don't know the answer!'*

It is impossible to convey on the page the effect Cooper achieved as he enhanced the telling of the story with mime, burlesque, audience acknowledgement and sheer physical effort. No wonder distinguished thespians like Hopkins, Gambon and Callow have such a high regard for him. However, he never became greedy with the principle. He was equally a master at simplification and concision, able to hone and perfect a joke until it was so streamlined it just had to connect with the audience.

What appeared in the Fun-Master archive as

```
Boy, am I burned up. Last night I must have slept like
   a log.  I woke up this morning in the fireplace!
```

became

Last night I slept like a log. I woke up in the fireplace.

Similarly

```
I ordered a broiled chicken and when the waiter brought it
   I noticed that one leg was smaller than the other. I
   told the waiter about it and he said "So what? You
   wanna DANCE with it?"
```

JUNGLEY!! - Big LION feeling insecure.

A big lion was suffering from a feeling of insecurity, and as he roared through the jungle one day he had this chip on his shoulder. Every animal he came across he'd stop them and say "Who is the King of Beasts?" and he was told that HE was. Finally he bumped into a mean, nasty-tempered elephant so he stopped him and said "Hey Jumbo, who is the King of Beasts?" so the elephant grabbed the lion with his trunk, tossed him into the air half a dozen times and then slammed him against a big tree. The lion picked himself up and said "Okay, but just because you don't know the ANSWER, you don't have to get SORE about it.'"

When I wrote *Always Leave Them Laughing*, my biography of the comedian, I set myself the task of transcribing the sequence exactly as it sounded and appeared in his act:

You know – the king of the jungle – the lion. And one day he woke up – he had a very bad temper – and he said to himself, 'I'm just going outside now and teach them all who's king of the jungle. Just to teach them.' So he gets up and he goes, 'Grrrrrr.' He was really mad, you know what I mean? 'Grrrrrr.' And he saw a little chimp and he said, 'You! Who's the king of the jungle?' And he said, 'You. You're the king of the jungle.' 'Well that's alright then. Alright.' And he walked along a bit more and he came across a laughing hyena and he said, 'Hey you, laughing boy.' And he went, 'Hah hah, hah hah hah. Hah hah, hah hah hah!' He said, 'Who's the king of the jungle?' 'Ooh, aah aah hah, ooh ooh aah, you are, you are.' So he walked on a little bit further and right at the very end was an elephant and a gorilla talking. And this gorilla looked at the elephant and he said, 'Here he comes, Jumbo. He's gonna do that "king of the jungle" bit again. He always does it.' He said, 'I'm not gonna stand it any more. I'm gonna leave you.' And he went up a tree. He said, 'I'll give you a trunk call later.' Hah hah hah! So he went up to this elephant and he said, 'Hey you. I'm talking to you, big ears.' He said, 'Who's the king of the jungle?' And this elephant got his trunk and wrapped it right round him and threw him up in the air and as he was up in the air coming down he was going, 'Who's the king of the jungle? Who's the king of the

He certainly would never have used these jokes for mainstream shows, innocent though they seem now.

FAMILY PLANNING!!

Once there was a couple who had 18 children. One day the husband said to his wife "No more kids." If you ever tell me you're gonna have another baby, I'll shoot myself." A year later, the wife said "Darling, I got news for you. We're gonna have another baby", so the husband grabbed his gun, went into the bathroom and put the gun to his head. Suddenly he stopped and said "What am I doing? I may be killing an innocent man."

LOVE BITES

A man awakened by his wife's crying, so he put the light on and went over to her side of the bed and asked her why she was crying. She said "You never kiss me goodnight anymore and I'm beginning to think you don't love me". He said, "Don't be silly, SURE I love ya" and he bent over and gave her a peck and said "NOW SHUT UP!" and around to his side of the bed he went and put the light out and went to sleep. She began to whimper again and woke him up. He said "NOW what's the matter with you?" She said "You call that a kiss? Some men bite their wives on the ear and the neck and all I get from you is a lousy peck". All of a sudden there was a terrific crash. His wife jumped up and yelled "What happened?" He said "You and your crazy ideas, I WAS LOOKING FOR MY TEETH!"

There is the inevitable emphasis (over-emphasis?) on wives (both generic and his own), members of the medical profession (medical, surgical and psychiatric), and members of the animal kingdom, not least dogs. He loved rambling animal stories with a delayed punch line. 'Shaggy dog' signifies the genre, although it usually featured beasts of larger size and fiercer disposition. Significantly he assigned the word 'Jungley!!' to same – the adjectival form and exclamation marks spelling out his special enthusiasm. On stage it was often in this category that he revealed his great gift for embellishing the material at his disposal. A typical 'shaggy dog' story featured the King of the Jungle. He originally typed it out as he found it in the American source:

WELL DRESSED

In a Nudist Colony there was one fellow wearing a
long beard and when he was asked what the idea of the
long beard was, he said "Well, SOMEONE'S gotta go out for
coffee."

for 'N for Nudist' or even 'C for Clothes,' where he has a joke where
the phrase 'well dressed' itself motivates the gag. 'Private Purposes'
is a somewhat limiting category for a joke that might have
been more easily found under 'P for Pub' or 'S for Sailor':

PRIVATE PURPOSES

Two sailors retired from the Navy and decided to
pool their savings and buy a saloon in a small town
and they started to paint it up and give it a real
good fixing inside and out. A few days later
after all the repairs were made, there STILL wasn't
any sign of an opening. One day a crowd began to
gather around the front and started yelling "HEY YOU
GUYS, WHEN ARE YA GONNA OPEN UP THIS JOINT?" One of
the sailors stuck his head out of the door and yelled
back "What dya mean, OPEN UP? Are you guys NUTS?
We ain't GONNA open up, we bought this joint for
OURSELVES."

Indeed, there was often no rhyme nor reason why a joke should be filed one way
or another. He had a category for 'Interior Decorator.' The lone joke filed here
could as easily have been placed under 'Psychiatrist,' while many of the gags
filed under the latter could have found refuge under other categories.

Interior decorator – Woman seeking advice

A woman went to an interior decorator and was having
a tough time getting what she wanted and finally
confessed to the Decorator that her husband think's
he's a BEAR. The Decorator said "A BEAR? Why don't
you go to a psychiatrist?" and she said "Do you think
HE can tell me what colour scheme to use in a CAVE?"

Most of the so-called 'R for Risqué' material is harmless enough, although
a few other categories stretch the imagination in the light of Cooper's
commitment to clean comedy: 'F' for Family Planning, 'L' for Love Bites.

a line he repeated often. And as he perused line after line he looked for the elements that spelt 'funny' to him – the play on words that rendered the obvious surprising, the visual quality that turned a joke into a cartoon of the imagination, the lateral thought that shed a quirky light on reality. He once confided, 'You have to have such innocent faith in a joke that the audience just has to laugh.' His words reinforce the fact that the selection procedure was no slapdash affair.

To many, the painstaking process that Tommy adopted will appear out of step with the idiosyncrasies of his stage character, but as one investigates the results of his efforts it is reassuring to discover instances where the old dysfunctional persona appears to shine through. 'A' for Animals, for Army and for Art speak for themselves, but then one encounters a category 'A for Actor-Cannons.' There cannot be many gags that feature both thespians and heavy artillery, but here we find one with a category all to itself, although one does wonder when and where he would have needed such a particular specimen. Its specification may well mean it was lost for all time as far as he was concerned. Now if he had filed it under 'A' for Actor or 'C' for Cannon…? For the record, here it is:

Actor - Cannons.

An actor got a job to fill in for a part and had to leave for Boston where the show was playing. All he had was one line "HARK! I HEAR THE CANNONS ROAR!" All day long he rehearsed the line, wherever he was, whether he was walking, eating or riding in the subway. All he kept repeating was "HARK! I HEAR THE CANNONS ROAR!" He finally got on the train to Boston and all the way he kept drumming the line into his head "HARK! I HEAR THE CANNONS ROAR". When he got to the theatre they were waiting for him. The show had already begun. He got dressed and on the stage he went, running the line through his head. All of a sudden came the time for his line and when the cannons went BOOM! he yelled "WHAT THE HELL WAS THAT?"

Other categories suggest a man struggling with a thesaurus. Why 'I' for Ignition and not simply 'Hot,' 'Heat' or 'Burning'? 'Well Dressed' seems a strange heading for a stray gag that was tailor-made (no pun intended)

Tommy never claimed an academic approach to the business of laughter in the way that some of his contemporaries were perceived. The brilliant Ken Dodd has been referred to as the slide-rule comic and may possibly have every book on laughter and its theory on his shelves. Bob Monkhouse could not have been far behind as a bibliophile and as he toured from show to show clung to two flight cases containing his scrupulously hand-written and illustrated joke books as if they were first folios of Shakespeare. Today the originality of the likes of Jimmy Carr, Harry Hill and Tim Vine owes much to an intellectual exercise in which words and concepts, logic and meaning collide with each other until the joke emerges fully formed. But, however the joke is achieved, its viability must always come down to a basic gut reaction. Cooper knew what would work for him. 'If it's funny, it's funny,' was

Once Tommy had inserted the joke in the A-Z file, another stroke of his ballpoint converted his original tick into a cross. In time he compiled an extraordinarily large and somewhat cumbersome system. At some stage he decided to upgrade the material by adding tabs that enabled him to read and access the categories more clearly. The task was never completed with the result that the full accumulation of material remains divided arbitrarily into two large sections, one with tabs and one with tabs pending. He also experimented for a while with typing individual gags on more conventional index cards, a process that surprisingly soon lost favour given the more compact nature of the format.

'Tape' constituted a reminder for the designated material to be rehearsed for his own experimentation into a reel-to-reel machine. 'Type' specified that the marked gags were destined for transcribing onto a sheet of A4 for eventual insertion into an elaborate A – Z index categorised by joke topic. This index also accommodated his choices from the bulkier volumes. Sometimes a subject would be assigned two sub-categories, marked 'P' and '1-L' accordingly. 'P' stood for Personal and '1-L' for One-liner. Thus under A for Army we find

> "P"
> ARMY
>
> ARMY   "PERSONAL"
>
> In the last war I fought and fought--but I had to go anyway.

in the first group and

> 1-L'S
> ARMY
>
> ARMY   ONE-LINERS
>
> If you wanna stay outta the Army   "JOIN THE NAVY"!

in the latter.

Likewise 'H' for Health yields

> "P"
> HEALTH
>
> HEALTH   "PERSONAL"
>
> I'm recovering from a cold---I'm so full of penicillin, that if I sneeze, I'll cure someone!

as well as

> 1-L'S
> HEALTH
>
> HEALTH   ONE-LINERS
>
> The best way to avoid a cold is to drink a lot of water. You never saw a FISH with a cold!

cabaret performance allowed him a tiny oasis of experimentation in which he vowed to try out a new gag or two. If the casualty rate was high, it is only because of the power of the tried and tested nature of his core material.

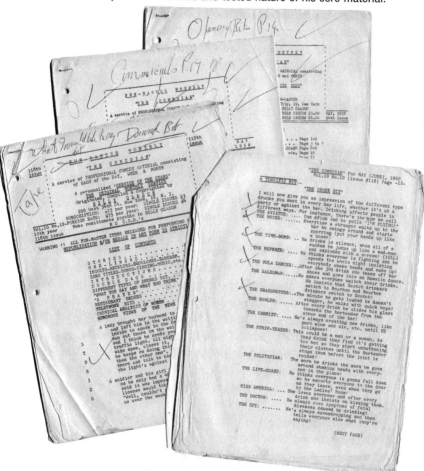

As he read each page, he marked the jokes that appealed with a tick. Sometimes he scrawled a specific reference or instruction on the front page of a joke bulletin. The two most frequent commands were 'Type' and 'Tape.'

interleaved with a heavier blank white sheet! Before long Tommy added in similar format to his shelves Glason's five-volume 'Book of Blackouts,' the nine sections of his 'Comedy and Emcee Lecture Book,' as well as the 'Humor-Dor for Emcees and Comedians.' Glason eventually progressed to mimeographing techniques and was able to circulate more of the same to a much wider clientele on a monthly basis in a gag-sheet called simply 'The Comedian.' Tommy signed up for this too, as he did for rival periodic publications like Art Paul's 'Punch Lines' and Eddie Gay's 'Gay's Gags.' Further material that sneaked its way into his files on a less regular basis comprised joke sheets by Pinkie DuFort and Vince Healy, vaudevillians all.

Upon Tommy's death this all amounted to a pile of paper almost twice as tall as the fez-capped giant himself. It is hard to believe that he ever read it all or needed much of it. But he did, on both counts. On the latter point, it was less a joke library for reference than an archive as security blanket. Every comedian lives in dread of the day when that tried and tested line fails to raise a laugh, tantamount to feeling the hand on your shoulder of the great joke-master in the sky calling in your comedy dues. But with a million or more gags to choose from, Cooper assumed he could sleep more soundly at night. That is, if he managed to get much sleep – he was determined to get his money's worth and made sure he read every joke from crumpled front cover to staple-snagged back page. He missed nothing and it is an indication of his seriousness to the joke that he was determined to take full advantage in this way over his rivals on the British comedy scene. What makes these aging reams so fascinating now is the process of selection and rehearsal they reveal. And it is here that we see the method in his madness again.

This book sets out to share with the reader the procedure Cooper employed in adapting this vast store of comedy for his own ends. It is likely that with the exception of the more risqué material reserved for stag events every single joke in these pages figured in his act at some stage, although obviously only a small percentage of them graduated to become the beloved almost-clichéd Cooper one-liners and shaggy dog tales that now contribute so vividly to his legend. He only needed so many of either, but every stage or

In a previous volume, 'The Tommy Cooper Joke Book,' I have explained his debt in this regard to the doyen of British stand-up comedians, Max Miller, as well as to his early reliance on the long series of soft-covered joke books compiled by the American gagster Robert Orben, which for a couple of decades winged their way across the Atlantic to the counters of the London magical depots where Cooper bought his tricks. Orben had been a magician and many of his lines were devised with their relevance to a particular piece of apparatus in mind. It was said that if for your fourteen shillings you used merely one joke out of the many included in the average forty or so pages, you got your money's worth. Cooper must have gained more value from them than anyone else. In time, his increased stature and earning power enabled him – and the television companies that employed him – to pay for custom-scripted material, from writers like Eddie Bayliss, Val Andrews and Freddie Sadler. But it is an accepted fact that no comedian feels he ever has enough material and Tommy was more voracious than most. On his first trip to America in 1954 he became familiar with the work of Billy Glason, an ex-vaudevillian who in his inevitable spare time on tour had compiled an index of every joke he ever heard on stage and every gag he was ever told off it. Upon retirement he set to and ordered everything he had gathered and much else besides into a series of home-produced publications obtainable only through limited subscription and at high prices. Ed Sullivan, Johnny Carson and Bob Hope all availed themselves of his service. Cooper was lucky to become his sole British client and in the process found himself the unofficial archivist in the UK for everything Billy produced.

Dominating this pile of material produced on flimsy typing paper in a pre-Xerox age were the twenty-six parts of the 'Fun-Master Encyclopaedia of Classified Gags.' The work was advertised at three thousand dollars, although Tommy was able to acquire the same for a knockdown price of nine hundred. Its high cost was determined by the strictly limited edition. How many copies can you achieve with a typewriter and carbon paper? Cooper's, which must have been at the end of the run, are only just legible, the thinnest paper being used 'to make it possible to make as many carbon copies as we can!' To make the print legible, each transparent wafer-thin page is

'Saving for Comedy's Rainy Day ... '

An introduction by John Fisher

It was no surprise to anyone who understood the dedication and attention to detail required by the master magician that there should be method in the madness of the most hysterical hocus-pocus man of all time. To create the continual illusion of incompetence in such a specialised area required an adroitness and split-second precision that rivalled the skills of any of the members of the 'now-you-see-it' brigade of which Tommy Cooper was both proud to be a member and yet astute enough to ridicule for his own greater popularity. But the laughter generated by his (sometimes) failed conjuring tricks was only half of the matter. Complementing his escapades with the bottle and the glass and the egg and the bag was a string of seemingly inconsequential patter ostensibly justified purely by the surrealism of its placing. One-liners, shaggy dog stories, visual puns and schoolboy howlers would be addressed to the audience with the seeming innocence and abandon with which he handled scarves, playing cards and all the other trademarks of the magician's trade. Cooper first responded to the sound of an audience's laughter at an early age when the milk that was supposed to stay in the upturned bottle cascaded to the floor of the shipyard canteen where he worked for part of his teenage years. From that moment the magic he targeted for his act was chosen for its comedy potential. As he progressed in the business, it was inevitable that he would need to segue into something approaching stand-up comedy if he did not wish to be pigeonholed on the cabaret and variety circuits as a mere speciality act. Hidden away in the innermost recesses of his Chiswick home at the time of his death was a secret hoard of jokes and gags that testified how important this consideration would prove to his success.

For Terry and Lynne Wright

and in memory of

Max Miller,

The Pure Gold of the Music Hall

TOMMY COOPER'S
SECRET JOKE FILES
JOHN FISHER